Jeremy's Airport

Airport
Jeremy's

JEREMY SPAKE

BBC

This book is published to accompany the television series
Airport which was first broadcast in 1998.
Executive Producer: Clare Paterson
Series Producer: Edwina Vardey
Producers: Edwina Vardey, Toni Williamson,
David Biddle, Sarah Neale
Assistant Producer: Sara Hardy

Published by BBC Worldwide Ltd,
Woodlands, 80 Wood Lane, London W12 0TT

First published 1998
Reprinted 1998
Copyright © Jeremy C. Spake 1998
The moral right of the author has been asserted.

The photographs were specially taken at Heathrow by Tino Tedaldi,
except for those on pages 10, 11, 14, 15 16, 63 and 84 which are copyright
of the author, and those on pages 48, 59, 114, 123, 134, 164 and 190.

Drawings of Jeremy by David Brown

ISBN 0 563 38459 X

Commissioning Editor: Sheila Ableman
Project Editor: Lara Speicher
Copy Editor: Barbara Nash
Designer: Linda Blakemore

Set in Janson by BBC Books
Printed and bound in Great Britain by Butler & Tanner Limited,
Frome and London
Jacket printed by Lawrence Allen Limited, Weston-super-Mare

CONTENTS

ACKNOWLEDGEMENTS

If you are one of the rare breed of people who actually enjoy reading the acknowledgement pages of books, you're no doubt familiar with the format. This is the part where the writer usually ends up thanking the entire world for their support. You know the sort of thing I mean, where thanks is given to the dustman for turning up on a Friday morning to collect all the discarded pages of a manuscript; not to mention the lollipop person (political correctness creeping in here) at the nearby school, who manages to slow down the noisy traffic while the frustrated writer struggles to meet the publisher's deadline.

Strangely enough, I'm no exception to this rather bizarre tradition, I truly would like to thank the world, or, at least, the people in it. After all, without the melting pot of passengers passing through Heathrow every day, my book would be very boring. So my first big thank you goes to you out there. Yes you … the agitated passengers, who systematically create chaos and mayhem every time you pass through the airports of the world. Without you, I, for one, would be lost.

No acknowledgements page, in my opinion, would be worthy of its name without a mention of the author's parents. If we're honest, without my parents there would be no Jeremy, and thus no *Jeremy's Airport* (flawlessly logical, I'm really sorry about that, folks). Thanks Mum and Dad for your support, especially Mum. I don't know how you managed to listen to every last word of my story with such enthusiasm and encouragement. I'd probably have fallen asleep after Day One.

People worthy of medals, simply for putting up with me, include my long-suffering comrades at Aeroflot. Pat, Kasia and Gabi have been especially supportive of my new-found recognition, and to them I cannot offer sufficient thanks.

My sincere gratitude is also extended to Barbara Nash, my guide and mentor, who demonstrated an almost infectious enthusiasm for *Jeremy's Airport*, without which I would have found it difficult to finish.

It is no mean feat to operate the world's busiest international airport as smoothly as Heathrow is run – for most of the time – so thanks to the landlords of Heathrow, BAA (who also assisted with the book), to all my colleagues in Terminal 2 and, of course, to Heathrow for existing in the first place!

A special note of thanks goes to Edwina Vardey and Sarah Neale of the BBC's Documentary Department, for their support and encouragement during the long dark periods I sat scratching my head, trying to work out why on earth I had allowed myself to be duped into being a part of the BBC's documentary *Airport*, which led to the writing of my book.

My final acknowledgement – yes, I know this is beginning to turn into an epic in its own right, apologies – goes to all the staff at BBC Worldwide for helping to make my book a reality. I would like to extend my extreme gratitude to Sheila Ableman, the Commissioning Editor, and to Lara Speicher, the Project Editor. When Sheila first suggested I write a book about my life at Heathrow, I thought she had just stepped off a long-distance flight and was suffering from a severe case of jet lag! Thanks, Sheila, I've discovered a few things about myself I didn't know.

*In loving memory
of my wonderful grandpa,
affectionately known by
me as Jeeves*

FASTEN YOUR SEAT BELTS

Into the Twilight Zone that's Jeremy's Airport

LADIES AND GENTLEMEN, welcome aboard. My name is Jeremy Spake and I'm your Traffic Services Supervisor from Aeroflot – Russian International Airlines. It will be my responsibility to guide you on your seven-day tour of the Twilight Zone – that is, Jeremy's Airport. Before we set off on our voyage of discovery, I should really tell you a little bit about myself and the remaining members of the crew, who will be on hand to assist you throughout the journey. However, I'd hate for you all to fall asleep before you've even had a chance to reach chapter one, so if you start to feel tired of my childhood tales, reach for the emergency exit and head straight for Monday, which, by the way, is rather logically the first chapter.

Me? Well … where do I begin? I'm fortunate enough to be the youngest of three children, which meant that Rose, my mother, had had plenty of time to practise her mothering skills on my two sisters, Nicola and Clara, before tackling the challenge of raising yours truly. Both my sisters are themselves now proud mothers, and their children are very much a part of my life. Clara is the family brain box, and is busy aspiring to become a teacher. She's one of those fortunate people in life who manage to succeed with the minimum of effort – don't you just hate it when someone is

✈ Yours truly, sporting my favourite Russian possession (and trademark), my trusty fur hat!

The family album:
Top left: My great-grandparents, lovingly known as Albert and Tessie.
Left: My grandparents, Stelenka and 'Jeeves'
Top centre: My dear grandmother Stelenka, standing on the banks of a lake, somewhere in northern Russia.
Above: The author aged, ooh, too young to say (about two and a half).
Above right: My mother Rose. This picture was taken in about 1959.

like that? Nicola and I have to work that much harder to achieve our ambitions, but hell, that can be fun too – life's not meant to be easy, or so they say.

What of my parents? Well, Barry, my father, was orphaned at the tender age of five and spent his formative years in various orphanages around Essex. Please don't get your handkerchiefs and violins out just yet, there is a happy ending, believe me. As a boy he dreamt of one day becoming a Formula One racing driver, to carry on the good fight started by the likes of Juan Fangio (Argentinian racing legend for those of you who haven't got a clue who he is) and Stirling Moss. Sadly, it was not to be, although when I sit in the car with him today, I'm not entirely convinced that he isn't still hankering after his childhood ambition. So, what did he do with his life? Simply, he went from steering wheel to helm, or, more precisely, the engine rooms of warships, becoming a successful naval career man, serving in Her Majesty's Royal Navy for more than twenty years. One thing we all inherited from my father was his gift of communication – he's the type of guy who could sell sand to the Arabs. Need I say more?

As a child, Rose, my wonderful mother (she did pay me to write that little accolade, so you'll have to forgive me) wanted to follow in the footsteps of Anna Pavlova, the world-famous prima ballerina. She set her sights on performing the ultimate Russian role of Odette from Tchaikovsky's *Swan Lake* no less. Much to my own disappointment, on account of my love for classical Russian ballet, her parents were unable to pay for the type of tuition required. Nevertheless, my mother achieved one of the greatest challenges in life – raising a family! Today she is kept busy as a civil servant, which is all far too boring to go into here. If we inherited the gift of the gab from Barry, our mother bestowed her intelligence and caring attitude upon us, something for which I'm personally very grateful. Thanks, Mum!

And last but not least, this clamber through my family tree would not be complete without mentioning my Russian granny – the one who, as you will discover, has the great privilege of waking me up at 4.30 a.m. for my early shifts. Due to her considerable influence, not only have I mastered her mother tongue (which, by the way, indirectly led to my working for Aeroflot), but I have also had instilled in me a love of all things Russian – and that includes big furry hats, as you will see.

I could go on about the family all day, given half a chance, but the story of my great ancestors is a book in itself, so back to me and the remaining members of crew on our voyage

Like most adolescent children, I had no idea what type of career I really wanted. At about the age of eleven, I developed a keen interest in journalism and quite liked the idea of being a foreign correspondent. However, during a lesson one day at school (a place I hated if the truth be known), I discovered that there would always be the possibility of having to report from war-torn countries, so I immediately decided to pursue other interests. I disliked almost all academic activities and had no real idea what to do about my future. Athletic, me? Never. So being a sportsman was clearly not on the cards. I was, however, delighted when I started taking drama classes. After just three lessons I was hooked and convinced that I would one day be a great actor (please forgive me – after all, this is childhood fantasy talking).

Acting ambitions soon vanished, however, after I spent one Sunday morning with my Father at Heathrow Airport. Sure, I'd been to airports before, but had never really thought about what was happening around me. Catching sight of a Russian-built IL62M of LOT, Polish Airlines, taking off for Warsaw stirred my imagination and I was sold on the idea of becoming an airline employee. Initially, like most boys interested in aircraft, I wanted to be a pilot, but soon found that my eyes and ears were about as much use as an ashtray on a motorbike and that I would therefore not make the A1 medical grade required. My passion was so great, however, that I decided to try for a job on the ground. Eventually, having overcome many obstacles, not least the distance I lived from Heathrow, I found myself working for British Airways.

Today, at the age of twenty-nine, I am charged with the task, albeit an almost impossible one, of controlling the smooth handling of seventeen weekly Aeroflot flights between Russia and the UK. The job involves liaising with our appointed handling agents at three London airports – Heathrow, Gatwick and Stansted – to ensure that service standards are maintained and that, whenever possible, our

More family pictures:

Top left: Everyone has a school photo like this lurking in a drawer. Some people don't seem to recognize me, so that's why there's a big pointer descending on my head!

Above: Me, Aunt Vera (my dad's sister), Mum and Dad. Lots of people think I look like Barry, although I would not want to admit this. The thought of growing older frightens me.

Far left: With my mother and sisters Clara (left) and Nicola. This picture was specially taken to send to my dad, who was busy on the high seas at the time.

Left: Me on a holiday in America in 1984.

This is me outside the smallest Aeroflot station in the world. It's in deepest Essex and also doubles up as my nephew's toy shed. We even get Siberian weather conditions in this part of the Aeroflot network!

aircraft depart on time. This, you will discover as you read on, is not as simple as it sounds. The majority of our flights operate with wide-bodied aircraft, which are basically aircraft with more than one aisle. The largest aircraft in our fleet, the Ilyushin IL86, seats 316 passengers in three classes, and the smallest, the Tupolev TU134, seats up 76 passengers in two classes. During the summer we have an average of 11,500 passengers travelling to Moscow and St Petersburg per month.

During the voyage through my seven-day shift we will be accompanied by some of my colleagues, who, you will soon learn, are just as mad as yours truly. There's cat-loving Pat, who has worked at Heathrow for more years than she cares to remember;. Harry, our Lionel Jeffries lookalike, who, in late 1997, celebrated his fiftieth year in aviation (now that clearly is insanity). (For those of you who have never seen Mr Jeffries in the film *Chitty Chitty Bang Bang*, I'm not about to describe the military-style chap he played, who seemed to spend most of his time in an outside toilet – time is precious you know!) You'll meet Igor, our engineer seconded from Moscow, whose Russian sense of humour keeps me going, but seems to confuse almost everyone else in the office.

There will, of course, be others, not least Kasia, our Polish empress, about whom I need say no more at present. So sit back, fasten your seat belt, ensuring that your tray and chair are in the upright position, and prepare for take-off. Oh, one last thing for those of you who are nervous travellers – the emergency exits to this book can be found at the front and back. Happy landings…

CHAPTER 1

CALM BEFORE THE STORM

SOME MIGHT ARGUE that being woken by one's granny at 4.30 a.m. on a Monday morning is the closest we are ever likely to get to hell. For me, however, Granny's early-morning call heralds the start of my favourite day of the week – yes, Monday! My sincere apologies to all of you who detest Mondays and find it difficult to cope with Monday-to-Friday, nine-to-five employment, but for me, Monday can be – and often is – a blessing because it's the quietest day of my working week.

Facing the daily drag of a 110-mile drive to work from my home just north-east of Colchester, Essex, I rarely find time to stop for breakfast. Even though at 5 a.m. my stomach's protesting at lack of nourishment, my brain convinces me that I need to get out on to the country's motorway system and do battle with the road-rage hordes if I'm to stand the remotest chance of making it to Heathrow in time for my 7.30 a.m. shift.

As one of the world's greatest people-watching fans – a good job really given the environment in which I work – I find there are invaluable lessons to be learned from the drive. It is often possible to draw comparisons between the motorists on the M25 and the passengers in Terminal 2.

Yours truly at work at Heathrow Airport. This is how I'm usually seen by passengers – on the move and in full flow!

Why do I never seem to be surprised by the selfishness of some drivers, who, for reasons known only to themselves, insist on driving in the outside lane of the motorway at 50 to 60 mph, successfully raising the blood pressure of everyone behind them? They seem oblivious to other road-users and intent on remaining in their own little worlds without the slightest consideration for others. It puts me in mind of some of the passengers I've met over the years, who insist that their 25-kilo piece of hand-baggage poses no threat to others' safety, and really will fit into the overhead baggage compartment on board the aircraft. Oh, Lord, if only they realized the error of their ways, life really would be so much simpler.

To most of my colleagues, the headache on a Monday morning is not the unfettered thoughtlessness of drivers on the M25, but the ones who manage to escape the grip of the motorway and make their way on to the M4-Heathrow slip road. At the end of this is the pair of tunnels that lead directly into the central area of the airport. Indeed, for most road-users this is the only means of reaching the very heart of Heathrow. More often than not, my colleague Patricia (known to me as Aunty Pat, on account of her wisdom), who lives in West Drayton (only a five-mile drive to work), spends far too much of her valuable time queueing on the slip road or in the tunnel, watching fellow drivers, who are, by and large, passengers late for a flight, trying desperately to beat the queue by weaving in and out of every little space that appears. Unlike Aunty Pat, my salvation is at hand in the shape of an airside driving licence and pass for my car – a perk of my job! (Airside is the part of an airport classified as being beyond Passport Control.)

Having managed to get past an inconsiderate driver in front of me on the M25, who is now frantically trying to jump ahead of the snake of traffic joining the M4, I head for the next junction, which takes me very conveniently to the cargo access tunnel, where my airside driving attributes come in handy. The cargo tunnel runs underneath one of Heathrow's three runways and emerges right next to my office in Terminal 2, so I'm able to arrive at work slightly less frayed than poor old Aunty Pat. Not that Pat *is* old you understand. I mean *old* in the sense of bosom buddies (he says, trying to dig himself out of a gaping hole).

As I switch on the office coffee-maker, I can hear Pat charging up the corridor determined to beat the 8.00 deadline for her to start work. Pat is just coming to
the end of six days on duty – six days that have seen her dealing with some particularly difficult situations, and the last thing she wants right now is to encounter me, full of the joys, at the beginning of my seven-day shift. (I'm still trying to work out the logic of our shift patterns, so please don't expect me to explain them to you. Suffice it to say, I shall be on duty for seven whole days.) None the less, I have just committed a cardinal sin and managed to wangle a weekend off.

'What kind of a weekend did you have, Aunty Pat?' There's no reply – just a grunt from the back of the office. 'Oh dear, we're out of sugar, Pat.'

Suddenly I seem to have stirred the animal in her, as she leaps into action. 'Oh, please don't say that, Jeremy,' she retorts. 'I refuse to survive Day Six without sugar!'

Knowing how close to the edge a lack of sugar can bring Pat, I decide to employ all my powers of ingenuity and pull a pile of those little airline catering packs out of my drawers – no, the ones in my desk, silly! You know the sort of thing I mean – those cellophane packs, with cutlery, that are almost impossible to open at 37,000 feet. They generally contain a sachet of sugar and one of those minute refreshing 'wipes', which I have often seen my father use as a substitute for a shower on a long journey. It must be his Royal Navy training that has led him to be so resourceful!

Having survived the first trauma of my duty by satisfying Pat's craving for sugar, I sit at my desk safe in the knowledge that Monday is, without doubt, the quietest day of the week for all of us working for Aeroflot at Heathrow. Unlike many European airlines operating from London, we enjoy a relatively quiet Monday, with just one rotation (when an aircraft arrives and departs on the same day) from Moscow and a night-stopping flight from Tokyo and Moscow, which stays on the ground until early on Tuesday morning.

'Shall I print off the daily report, or have you already done it?' comes the somewhat more relaxed voice of Pat from the kitchen. 'I've already done everything for today, love,' I call back, 'although I couldn't be bothered to get off my fat one to unlock the office door for the passengers, so if you wouldn't mind … cheers ears.'

The daily report is our battle plan from which we gather info on how many passengers to expect, whether they are just travelling to Moscow or transiting, and, perhaps more importantly for the passengers, whether or not they are vegetarians, etc. If I had a fiver for every passenger who arrives at check-in stating that they had requested vegetarian meals only to find they haven't got them, I would be a very wealthy man and probably wouldn't be writing this book. Sadly, I tend to look at the completed daily report with considerable apprehension. I can tell an awful lot about the kind of day I'm going to have just by looking at this single sheet of A4 paper. Ridiculous as this may seem, it's true.

Glancing at today's, I am comforted to learn that the myth about Mondays is not about to be shattered. We are expecting 150 or so passengers travelling mainly to Moscow. This generally means Russians, who are, by and large, a delight to work with; and, yes, I am biased on account of the fact that my mother's half of the family originates from that mighty land, and, thanks to her and my other Russian relatives, I am bilingual. To my delight, I'm able to declare: 'We only have two transit passengers today, Pat,' and can hear the instant relief in her voice as she replies, 'Yeah.' It's not that I want you to think that we have an aversion to transit passengers, but they do cause unique problems, which will become apparent as you read on.

09:20 The aura of peace encircling my desk is broken by the phone ringing. This, in itself, is no great event, but you must understand that one bad phone call can upset you for the rest of the week. Reaching for the receiver with some trepidation, I find myself recalling a Christmas Day when a female staff passenger from a far-flung place telephoned to ask: 'Will I have any problems getting to Delhi in March?' Given that none of us really wants to work at Christmas, the last thing you expect is a member of staff to ring up and upset you with an inane crystal-ball-type question. How could I possibly know of any problems that might affect flights three months down the line? Naturally, ordinary passengers can be forgiven for making such enquiries on Christmas Day, or any other day come to that, but, I ask you, a staff passenger! Shouldn't staff have a bit more sympathy for hard-done-by colleagues who find themselves working on Christ's birthday? Anyway, suppressing the obvious retort, I replied: 'I'm sorry, but today *is* Christmas Day and our reservations department, which deals with advance travel queries, *is* closed. They will re-open on Monday and I'm sure *they* will be only too pleased to assist you further. *We* deal only with EMERGENCIES here at Heathrow.' 'You're not a very kind gentlemen, are you?' the lady snapped. 'I worry very much about chance. My family, for example, may be ill and I need to know now that all will be okay.' As you can imagine, thoughts started spinning through my head, like: Am I supposed to be Aeroflot's equivalent of Mystic Meg? Or is it simply my bad luck to get such a crackpot caller on Christmas Day?

Returning to the matter in hand – the phone now ringing on my desk – my initial fears are allayed by a calm voice at the other end of the line. 'Hi there! It's British Airways in Terminal 4 here. Do you have anyone who speaks Russian available? We're having a few problems with a group of transit passengers.'

Being a sucker for a sob story and always wanting to act as a knight in shining armour for damsels in distress, I proudly declare, 'Ooh, your luck's in, hon. I can translate for you. What's the problem?' Why, oh why, do I always let my heart rule my head? Sense dictates that you should establish what the problem is *before* volunteering to do anything – especially at Heathrow – but yours truly, being a bit of a fool, jumps in feet first.

'The passengers have just arrived from South Africa and are in transit to Berlin. Could you explain that they need to follow the signs for the Flight Connections Centre?' 'Sure, no problem. If you put one of them on the phone, I'll have a word with them.' Phew, a near escape, but there is nothing complicated about explaining what the group needs to do next. *'Alyor eto Aeroflot,'* I say, which tells the Russian at the other end of the line that he's talking to Aeroflot. *'Oi! Dobri Den u nas malenkaya problema,'* replies the passenger, clearly delighted at being able to speak Russian for the first time in a fortnight.

But then my heart begins to sink as the caller declares that he has a small problem. Anyone familiar with Russians will confirm that what Russians deem to be a 'small problem' often turns out to be the very opposite. Anyway, the group had already understood the need to go to the Flight Connections Centre but were having trouble explaining to the British Airways staff that, because of a check-in error, their baggage had only been checked through to London, *not* all the way to Berlin, their ultimate destination. And, regretfully, the group did not have visas for Britain, which meant that they were unable to proceed through Passport Control to the baggage hall in order to retrieve their luggage.

Knowing that each passenger, when checking in, is given an individually numbered receipt, otherwise known as a tag in the industry, which should make detecting a bag easier, and noting a hint of distress in the passenger's voice, I say in Russian: 'Could you give me the numbers of your baggage tags and any information concerning the type of bags and their colour?' 'Well,' the passenger replies, 'that's not very convenient. I will have to ask everyone in the group to describe their bags. Where are the bags anyway?' he adds, the tone in his voice changing to that of a hungry lion.

Trying to explain that I do not work for BA and that I am simply trying to help them out somehow does not seem a viable option at that precise moment. If truth be known, I haven't a clue where their luggage is, but am assuming that it is merrily whizzing around the carousel in the baggage hall of Terminal 4. (I'm keeping my fingers crossed that this is the case, as I do not much relish informing the passenger that the baggage is still in Cape Town, where they checked in, which, at this stage, cannot be ruled out.)

Now, I hear you asking yourself, how difficult can it be to find a few bags that have gone astray? Well, in theory, it is not at all difficult. But when you are dealing with thousands of bags every day, experience soon tells you that practice does not necessarily make perfect, and that bags can – and do – seem to vanish into thin air. I'm already beginning to dread the thought of explaining to the group that they will have to fly on to Germany in the uncertain knowledge of their luggage's whereabouts.

Thankfully, however, there is a god – or at least someone who is on the ball at British Airways. The airline's Baggage Services team in Terminal 4 has already located the luggage and assures me that it is winging its way along a specially constructed baggage conveyor belt that links Terminal 4 with Terminal 1, to be loaded on to the passengers' connecting flight.

The need for me to beg forgiveness on behalf of BA has been dispelled and I can pass on the good news to the passenger. 'They've managed to locate your bags and have already put them on to the connecting flight for you.' The passenger, in almost stereotypical behaviour, hangs up without offering a word of thanks. Still, life can be a bit like that at Heathrow – our efforts on behalf of others often go unappreciated.

As I hang up, I can't help but notice that the pile of paperwork that has landed on my desk over the weekend looks somewhat reminiscent of K2 or Everest (yes, I am exaggerating a bit to get the sympathy vote). I'm finding it difficult to summon up the energy to attack its grand face and decide instead to wander down to check-in, leaving Pat chatting with Kasia, who has just started duty.

Kasia, a Passenger Services Officer, is one of our Polish contingent, who is lovingly known by a variety of names, not least the 'Tsaritsa of Gubnoi Pomadi' (which means, for all of you who failed O-Level Russian, the Empress of Lipstick). If Kasia were to confess to a crime, it would have to be to the excessive application of lipstick during the average working day. Given half a chance, I am convinced that my aristocratic Polish colleague could single-handedly keep Lancôme, Helena Rubinstein and others like them, in business. On the rare occasion when I'm bored, I try imagining what Kasia would look like without her war paint.

On my way to check-in I receive a reminder of how lucky we are at Aeroflot to have a relatively quiet Monday. Peeping across the concourse at my col-leagues on the Swissair ticket desk, I see the remains of a bedraggled staff who have just finished dealing with the early Monday morning businessmen, who are always in a rush to get away to their important

meetings. The staff all look as though a herd of elephants has just trampled over them, and I can't help feeling relieved that I'm not one of them.

Passing them like the cat who's got the cream – after all, I've not yet been through the mill of verbal abuse (it still being early days) – I utter the greeting, 'Morning. How's it going?' as though I can't tell just from looking at them. 'Oh, the usual,' one of them replies. 'How are you?' For the life of me, I don't know why, I always say, 'Oh, surviving – as you do.' But it strikes me as I reply that it's a bit soon into my shift to be 'surviving'. I should be *winning* this early on.

'Tell me, where can I check in for the flight to Tashkent?' comes the rather curt voice of a well-dressed German businessman, who, like many other passengers, has spotted my security pass and made the correct assumption that I work at Heathrow. 'I'm terribly sorry, sir,' I answer, 'but you're either a day too early, or a day too late. Uzbekistan Airways don't have a flight on a Monday. But there is a service to Tashkent on a Tuesday evening at around 21.30, and their staff are normally here about three hours before the flight's departure.' (Uzbekistan is a former Soviet Republic and current member of the Commonwealth of Independent States. The country was at the heart of the ancient Silk Road and is now one of world's largest producers of cotton. Sorry, readers, I don't want to bog you down with irrelevant bits of information, but I simply can't help myself where the former Soviet Union is concerned. I can only hope that you will indulge my greatest passion.)

Meanwhile, I have noticed an instantaneous change in the passenger's body language. I've been on a fair few body-language courses over the years and usually arrive on Day One with that feeling of been there, done that, got the T-shirt. But I never cease to be amazed by the instructor's inability to make a passenger raising his fist as aggressive as it is in reality. 'I have just arrived from Munich and wish to check in. Where is Uzbekistan Airways?'

✈ Here you see the organized chaos of Aeroflot's office, Kasia listens in as I converse with my colleague Pat about another incident at the departure gate, 'Yes, it was this big and this thick, and he insisted it was for his own personal use!!'

You've guessed it – I've been talking to myself! It comes as no surprise to me that the passenger sees nothing strange in trying to check in almost thirty-six hours before the flight is due to leave. However, I can't help but wonder who has misinformed this unfortunate man. 'Well, sir,' I try again, 'to my knowledge, as I have tried to explain, Uzbekistan Airways does not have a flight until tomorrow evening.' 'That's not good enough,' booms the mighty voice of the businessman, who, given time, could certainly compete with Chancellor Kohl for the role of Powerful Voice of Germany. 'Where is their manager?'

Do I give up here and now and just pretend that we have not been having one of those circular conversations? You know the type – where two people *seem* to be speaking to each other, but one of them is not really listening to what is being said and seems to be stuck in a groove. Well, as many of my colleagues will confirm, these types of conversations are not unusual at Heathrow. I decide to plod onwards and upwards with Chancellor Kohl's replacement. 'Maybe you would like to contact their handling agent – Aer Lingus – who I'm sure will assist you further.' 'No. I want to see the Uzbekistan Airways' manager. Where is their office?'

I feel like asking one of the staff to give me a pinch just to confirm that I am in fact at work and *not* in one of those Japanese torture game shows you see on telly. Sure enough, I am standing right next to our own Aeroflot check-in desks, which need to open in less than five minutes, irrespective of my German friend and non-existent flights to Tashkent. 'I'm terribly sorry, sir, but, as I have tried to tell you, Uzbekistan Airways is not open at the moment. I really do need to be getting on. I am sure the Aer Lingus girls will offer you some advice.' With a piercing stare, the passenger bids me farewell in typical fashion: 'So there is no flight today?' They never seem to give up, do they! 'I'm afraid not, sir. But I do hope you manage to sort your problem out and get away okay. Uzbekistan really is a beautiful country.'

It's just 10.30 in the morning and I've already had to run the gauntlet with someone else's passengers. Thankfully, I find these types of experiences excellent warm-ups and now feel fully prepared for my own jet-setters.

At check-in, there is already a considerable queue of passengers for the 1.30 flight, mostly Russians, which, given how patient they are, is no bad thing, as we appear to have only two of the four desks operational. 'Where's the CLO?' is my first question. The CLO is the check-in co-ordinator, who should be liaising with me and the rest of the Aeroflot staff, ensuring that our service standards are met. 'Not too sure. I think she popped off to the COP.'

Sorry, folks, this is beginning to sound like a Harry Palmer spy novel where you have to try to remember about forty coded names and acronyms. Unfortunately, the airline industry is no stranger to codes and uses them all the time. To compound the issue, not only do airlines use the industry's standard codes, but they also seem to develop their own, and our handling agent is no exception. The COP is the control room from where AFSL (oops, another acronym – Air France Servisair Limited) co-ordinates all its passenger service staff.

'Hi there!' I say, ringing through. 'It's the superior Russian airline here. Is there any chance of opening another desk to be going on with? My passengers are beginning to foam at the mouth a bit.' 'Morning Jeremy, the staff are already on the way to you!' comes the predictable reply. I should explain that when people start working in our industry, the first thing they have to learn to say is: 'They're on the way,' and say it in such a tone as to sound totally convincing. The other miracle phrase that seems to roll so easily off the tongue around Heathrow is: 'They left at least five minutes ago and should be with you shortly.' Both these seemingly harmless phrases can spell trouble. Invariably, what is meant is that no one is on the way and that someone somewhere is going to spend the next twenty minutes frantically trying to find a free staff member to send.

The delightful Shirley at AFSL is not, however, lying to me. Just as I go to put the phone down, two members of staff come round the corner with the CLO. 'Shirley,' I drawl, 'once again you have shattered my illusions about this place. Cheers, love. I'll speak to you soon no doubt.'

✈ OVERLEAF The check-in area can often prove to be somewhat stressful, especially when a flight is full and all the passengers have their full quota of baggage. However, on this occasion I can take time out to chat with a couple of the passengers.

Check-in can now commence in earnest. A group of Russian athletes is eagerly chomping at the bit to do so, but appears to be causing
a few puzzled looks on the faces of the staff. '*Shto sluchilos?*' (What's
wrong?) I ask in Russian in an authoritative voice. 'Sorry, I don't speak
English,' comes the reply. Have I missed something here, or did I just
ask him in Russian – *not* English – what's wrong? Finally, the penny
drops and the group leader apologizes for his stupidity (which always
bodes very well with me) and explains that one or two of the passengers might have a few kilos too many.

Putting his mind at rest, I say: 'Please don't worry. We can check
you all in together, which means that we will take the combined weight
of all the baggage. If this is within your collective allowance of 280
kilos (there being fourteen passengers each permitted 20 kilos), there
will be nothing to pay. If you are slightly over, I'll be happy to discuss
the options'. 'Fine. Could you explain that to your girl? She might not
want to do it like that,' replies the burly weight-lifter, who is the type
of guy you wouldn't want to argue with. 'No problem,' I reply. 'She
will be delighted as it makes her life so much easier. Ms Brown,' I call
with that *Are You Being Served?* note in my voice, 'could you check 'em
all in together and pool the baggage?' 'No problem, Jeremy,' she
replies, 'but could you just ask them the security questions – my
Russian's a bit rusty. Thanks.' Ms Brown, known to all her friends as
Nicola, is a delightful member of the AFSL staff and a real pleasure to
work with, so I'm happy to ask those all-important security questions
on her behalf.

Having successfully managed to check in our fourteen athletes, and
established that they are only 15 kilos over the permitted 280, Nicola
asks, 'Jeremy, what do you want to do about the excess?' 'Don't worry
about it, Nicola,' I reply. 'I'm sure you haven't got the energy after all
that checking in to explain to them how to get to the ticket desk to pay
for excess.' Breathing a sigh of relief, Nicola hands the group leader all
the boarding cards.

✈ I try to compose myself as I look at the scales, which are confirming,
once again, that baggage is the bane of my life. The number of people who do
not understand that 20 kilos is 20 kilos and that anything over will cost them!

As is standard practice, she also explains that they need to go upstairs to the first floor, through Passport Control and then watch the screens for the boarding gate number to come up. Simple? Well, yes, if you speak English, but our group has grasped only the essentials of the language, such as thank you, sorry, smoke, etc. I'm sure, like us, *everybody* understands what is meant by first floor, don't they? Wrong. To a Russian, the first floor is, in fact, the ground floor, and if you want them to go to the *English* first floor, you have to make absolutely certain that you ask them to head for the *Russian* second floor. Confused? Well, try telling 316 passengers on a packed flight – *that's* confusing!

I move on to my next problem, which turns out to be an elderly passenger who wants a seat with leg room, no children anywhere near it and as far away from smokers as possible. Seeking light relief for just a moment, I excuse myself and return to explaining to the athletes what to do next. Suitably revived, I turn back to the elderly lady: 'Madam, it really isn't a problem to find you a seat with leg room away from smokers, but as far as keeping children away from you, there is not a lot I can do about that.'

The Margaret Rutherford lookalike is grateful for my compassionate tone, but retorts: 'Really, young man … Do you mean to tell me that in this day and age you cannot keep children away from me? In my day …' 'Well, madam,' I say soothingly, 'the flight is not full and I am sure you will be able to move, should you find an excessive number of small children are surrounding you.' As I call for a wheelchair, our elderly passenger seems content that we have at least succeeded in meeting some of her requests.

11:48 My radio is hissing away underneath my jacket. 'Two-four-one in the zone for Golf 12,' yells Aunty Pat above the noise of the phones ringing in the office. More code, I'm afraid. Two-four-one is the incoming flight number from Moscow, and the word 'zone' is magic-like music to my ears. This means the aircraft is just ten to fifteen minutes from landing at Heathrow and that, when it lands, it will be going to parking stand G12 (we use the phonetic alphabet in the airline industry). 'Copied [our word for message received]. I'm off to the gate to meet the arrival.'

Just as I finish replying to Aunty Pat, I spot the Tsaritsa coming towards me, looking resplendent in her freshly applied lipstick. 'Kashinka,' I call, 'there's nothing much happening down here at the moment. We seem to have checked in most of the Economy Class passengers, although there is one guy over there trying to reduce his baggage.' 'What have you agreed with him?' asks Kasia. 'Well, I said if he can keep his hand luggage to no more than 7 kilos, I will allow him 25 kilos of hold baggage. I'm not that optimistic, though, as he originally had 45 kilos of hold and a paltry 15 kilos of hand. Good luck! I'm off to the gate.'

Leaving Kasia at check-in to wade her way through the remaining passengers, I head for Central Staff Search. This is the area where staff pass from the landside area of the airport into the security-sensitive airside zone, which I think of as the Twilight Zone. Strange things seem to happen airside at airports, things that make the *X Files* seem positively tame by comparison. Airside is definitely like nowhere else on Earth.

Entering the Central Staff Search area, I always feel like Mr Ben – a cartoon character who used to be on children's television when I was a boy. He'd go to a fancy dress shop, enter the changing rooms and come out in a completely different world. But, unlike Mr Ben's new environment, Central Staff Search is an extremely unpleasant area sandwiched between two sets of toilets, with no windows and an air-conditioning system that could transform the Sahara Desert into the Siberian Plains in winter.

Without stopping (which is very unusual for a chatterbox like me), I pass straight through the Central Staff Search area, saying to my colleagues in security, 'Can't stop, guys, I'm in a bit of a hurry. My aircraft is just about to go on to Golf 12.' As a person who loves to chat, which has never ceased to amaze my mum on account of me refusing to speak to anyone but her up to the age of three and a half, it is always difficult to cut colleagues dead. However, when needs must, I seem to find the willpower and resist the temptation.

Rushing down the corridor, not pausing to admire the second set of toilets (!), I enter the wonderful world of the airside Duty Free shopping mall. Shopping at airports has taken on a whole new meaning since the beginning of the 1990s, and, in Terminal 2, in addition to buying the usual booze and fags, you can now browse around the local branch of Harrods and eat a fresh salmon lunch at a fancy fish bar.

Having no time to immerse myself in the ambience, I press on towards Gate 12. Turning the corner, I bump into one of my closest friends – my old boss, Dave Thomas. Dave is the Station Manager of CSA, Czech Airlines, and having been with CSA for over thirty years, has the honour of being Heathrow Airport's longest-serving Station Manager.

Such good friends are Dave and I (this might have something to do with the fact that we share the same birthday), that I often find myself seeking refuge in his house after a bad day at work, when I simply can't face the long drive home. I am known to him – and most of my close friends at work – as the General Secretary of the Party, and as such I always need to make time to listen to their problems. However, time is running out and the aircraft can't be far off from landing. 'Sorry, Dave, can't stop,' I explain. 'I can hear the aircraft on stand and I'm already chasing my tail this morning.' 'Don't worry, mate,' Dave replies in his usual friendly manner. 'I'll perhaps see you in the office later on this afternoon.' 'Fine, just make sure there's plenty of water in that kettle of yours,' comes my out-of-breath reply.

There she is, the Ilyushin IL86, the biggest aircraft in Aeroflot's fleet and one of my favourites. The aircraft was originally designed to carry 350 passengers, but in our current three-class configuration we have seats for 316 people. The aircraft door is just opening. '*Privyet!*', I say, using the informal Russian equivalent of hello. I know Tanya, the Chief Stewardess, very well. She's a stunning woman who has a charming way with everyone. '*Privyet! Kak ty pozhivaesh?*' Tanya replies, choosing one of the many possible greetings in Russian. 'Life for me at the moment,' I answer, 'is pretty good, thanks. How many passengers are on board, Tanya?'

Yes, I do already know from all the telexes I have received from Moscow just how many people boarded the plane, but it is always

✈ 'Dave, smile for the camera, or else!'. One of my greatest friends, Dave Thomas, knows better than to ignore the words of the General Secretary when given a direct order.

worth double-checking. 'One hundred and eighty-seven. Here are all the docs.' 'Thanks, Tanya. It's okay for the passengers to disembark.' I hand all the documents to my colleague from AFSL, who, in turn, will distribute them to the relevant people, such as Cargo and the Royal Mail.

Standing patiently while the incoming passengers leave the aircraft, I begin to switch into my aircraft departure mode, which, on certain days, can terrify all the staff around me, especially if the aircraft has arrived late. I get a real buzz when challenged by a late incoming flight, and, being very fussy, demand great things of the staff around me. Today, however, is not one of those days, so even the cleaning staff can feel safe from the wrath of Khan.

Cleaning an aircraft is very time-consuming and, when time is of the essence, the speed with which a cleaning crew does the job can mean the difference between an aircraft leaving on time or leaving late. For some reason that I can't fathom (!) the cleaners always have a particular look in their eyes when they spot me coming. 'Okay, lads? I need you off the aircraft by 12.45 so there's plenty of time.' 'Yeah. No probs. We'll be finished sooner than that,' says the cleaning supervisor, who by this time has made a quick readjustment of his expression and managed to wipe the stressed look from his face.

Back upstairs at the departure gate, passengers have been filing in nicely. 'I can tell it's Monday,' I say to the boarding-gate staff. 'The aircraft has arrived on time, the passengers are virtually all checked in and, miracle of miracles, the cleaners seem to be finishing on time.' By saying this I am trying to convince the staff that things are going swimmingly well. Yes, at the moment they are, but you never can tell … 'Can you confirm the boarding time for us?' asks Tom the team leader. 'On the hour at 13.00, Tom. You don't need to worry about the flight announcements, I'll do them myself.'

Crackle, crackle, pop! 'Jeremy – from Kasia … *Helloooooo*,' Kasia's on the radio, but which of the six radios that have been dumped on the desk is *my* radio? 'Go ahead, Kashinka,' I say, sorting it out from its fellows. 'We've finished down here with 153 passengers plus one infant.' By uttering these words, Kasia confirms that it *is* Monday. It's only 12.55 and check-in has closed five minutes early. Bliss.

'Okay, Tom, let's go boarding. Can you just make sure that the elderly passenger at the end of the lounge is pre-boarded [put on the aircraft first]. I  want to be certain that she's happy with her seat. She was very precise at check-in about the kind of seat she wanted.'

Luckily Clare, the agent who checked in our Margaret Rutherford lookalike, is at the gate, so Tom asks her to escort the lady to the aircraft ahead of the mad rush. 'Jeremy,' Clare says on her return, 'she's delighted. There aren't too many children, her seat is in exactly the right place, but she hopes there won't be a draught round her legs during the flight.' I take comfort in the knowledge that at least one passenger is happy with my efforts.

All's well … almost. The guy at check-in with too much baggage has got his act together and managed to pay some of the excess baggage charge, but he's still not happy. At the gate he corners me and asks, 'Why are you charging me excess? I left Moscow with the same amount of baggage and wasn't asked to pay any charges.' Here we go again … If I have had this conversation once with a passenger, I've had it a thousand times. 'Well,' I commence, 'I obviously cannot comment on the situation in Moscow, sir, as, regretfully, I was not present when you left Russia. However, I do know that my colleagues in Moscow are as tough at implementing standard regulations as we are. We're not averse to helping passengers out, but I'm afraid I cannot allow you to take 60 kilos of baggage free of charge, given that you are only entitled to 25 kilos, including hand baggage.'

'That's bloody typical,' our overweight passenger retorts. 'You're all the same, you people. You just love being able to wave your authority all over the place.' 'Sir, believe me,' I protest, 'I apply the same rules to every passenger. You are *not* being singled out for victimization. Upsetting passengers is *not* something I enjoy, but I do need to keep the interests of everyone in mind at all times.'

As the passenger trundles off towards the aircraft muttering obscenities under his breath, as is often the way with passengers, I recall a previously unheard of chain of events that had taken place several weeks earlier. Graham, the Station Representative of Adria Slovenian Airlines, had encountered a similarly unpleasant individual,

who was also, the individual claimed, the victim of an over-zealous, power-crazed airline employee. In an almost carbon copy of today, Adria's passenger had also been particularly rude and failed to understand the need for him to pay excess baggage charges. Nothing unusual in this. But early one morning Graham had looked at me, shock registering on his face, saying: 'Jeremy, you're never going to believe this!' 'Try me.' 'D'you remember the guy I told you about the other day – the one with the excess? The one who was particularly unpleasant? Well, he's just rung from Sarajevo and apologized for being so obnoxious.'

Picking myself up off the floor, I could not, initially, think of anything to say (which has to be a first in the history of Jeremy). I blurted out, 'You're joking! Not only do you get a passenger apologizing for their obvious rudeness, but they do it from Sarajevo!' Needless to say, Graham spent the rest of that day in a state of shock.

'Tanya, that's everyone – 153, plus a baby.' Tanya confirms that all is in order and bids me farewell. Looking at my watch I am delighted to see that it's 13.27 and the doors have closed three minutes ahead of schedule. 'Well done everyone. I'm not going to tempt fate by praying to God that the rest of the week will be as smooth.' Tom, who by now is printing off all my passenger lists, remains silent, knowing that answering me – and possibly creating an error while he does so – could jeopardize his week as well.

Returning to the office at a slightly more leisurely pace, I take the opportunity to chat with a few people. 'Jeremy, where are you?' Lordy lord, my  radio is at it again. It's Aunty Pat, who has now developed the distinct tremor in her voice that comes to all of us after a long tour of duty. 'I'm coming, Pat,' I say to reassure her I've not been delayed for any troublesome reason. 'I'm just heading towards the Tardis.'

✈ 'Can you hear me, Mother?' I cautiously approach the microphone to make the all-important boarding announcement, never knowing whether the passengers will actually listen, or simply kill me in the stampede. 'There's a seat for everyone! No need to rush!'

As a rule, I head back to the office via Passport Control and the baggage hall just to make certain there have been no problems for our arriving passengers, but the tremor in Pat's voice leads me to take the short cut via the Tardis – a glass cylinder next to Terminal 2's Passport Control that regulates the flow of staff back to the landside area of the building. At the Tardis, staff swipe their security passes through a special de-coder and then enter this glass sarcophagus to momentarily escape the clutches of the Twilight Zone.

Entering the Tardis is always a lottery – one never knows when one's time will be up. Feeling like Captain Kirk on the *Starship Enterprise* when he is beamed to lands afar, I enter the capsule. Oh, Lord! The alarm is sounding. I'm trapped. 'Oh, God, *please* don't do this to me. I'm having such a wonderfully peaceful day!'

In the distance beyond the X-ray machines, I can just see the security supervisor coming to release me from captivity. By now, there is also a queue of staff wanting to access the Tardis. I try to attract the queue's attention by banging gently on the glass, 'Hello! *HELLO!*' People are trying to disguise the fact that they are irritated by the delay, but amused by the hostage-like situation in front of them. '*HELLO!* HELP! *Please* tell him to hurry!'

There's no way anyone's done research on how much oxygen a person has in here, and thus what my life expectancy could be. 'You all right in there?' quips the security man. 'Oh, fine and dandy. Sort of thing I like to do – get stuck in a fish bowl that's on display to the world.' After an eternity the door opens and releases me. Pat is still calling to establish where I have vanished to.

Thankfully I am not on duty for the night arrival at 19.45, so I decide to make the most of Monday's bliss and head for home early at 14.30. Pat follows hot on my heels, a look of complete exhaustion on her face. 'Two days off now, Aunty Pat,' I say cheerily. 'What are you planning to do, other than sleep?' Pat now hanging on to the edge of life, whispers: 'I want to finish decorating my hall'.

I arrive home just after 17.00 to be met by my cat, Lenin, a handsome grey beast, who has spent most of the day outside and is now eager to be fed. Monday is virtually over, and it's all downhill from here, isn't it?

✈ In my next life I have decided to come back as one of those shop dummies – I've had plenty of practice standing behind glass! Here, I'm in the Tardis, waiting for Scottie to beam me up.

CHAPTER 2

IT'S ALL DOWN- HILL FROM NOW ON

AS A CHILD I FELL IN LOVE WITH, and developed an obsession for, commercial airliners. Whenever my parents suggested a family excursion, I would endeavour, much to the disappointment of my two sisters, to make sure that there was at least one location with aircraft on the itinerary. Thoughts of those childhood years came flooding back to me this morning as a small Piper twin-propeller aircraft flew past me into the sunrise. The sight of an aircraft flying towards the sun is always romantic in itself (well, it is for me!), but a sighting at 4.40 a.m. while driving along the M25 is a nostalgic reminder of why I chose to work in the less-than-logical world they call the airline industry.

Reaching Heathrow, any thoughts of nostalgia are instantly replaced by more pressing concerns about the day ahead. We have two flights to Moscow on a Tuesday, and the first is due to leave in just under three and a half hours, at 9 a.m. As I pass through one of the many CPs at the airport (sorry, these codes are really taxing, I know – CP, meaning Control Post, is Heathrow Airport Limited's way of saying Security Check Point), I can see our European-built Airbus A310 parked on stand Echo 40.

Just checking that all meals, drinks and bread rolls are on board before passengers embark for flight SU581 to Tokyo via Moscow.

TUESDAY

45

On my way to the office, I take a short detour via the aircraft to check all is well. I can remember arriving at Stansted Airport early one morning to the news that a truck-driver had reversed into the wing of an ageing BAC 1-11 jet during the night. However, that sort of thing is extremely rare, and this morning everything's hunky-dory on stand Echo 40, so I head to the office to prepare for the day's onslaught.

I open the office door to a chorus of three phones warbling and our computers merrily regurgitating the daily report, which tells me it is going to be a busy day. I can only deduce from all this activity that our subs for electricity are fully up to date.

The first task I tackle is to call catering to confirm how many meals will be needed for our first flight. Trying to eliminate any possibility of delay is the main role for any of us in the office, so fully briefing catering, which is situated several miles from the airport, is absolutely essential. Today the staff need to arrive at the aircraft in less than two hours with 180 fully prepared hot passenger meals, 13 crew meals, 40 litres of drinking water, 20 kilos of ice, enough tea and coffee for everyone, not to mention lemons and a whole host of other items that passengers have come to expect over the years. 'The aircraft,' I confirm, 'is on Echo 40. Okay?' 'That's fine,' comes the always pleasant reply of one of the girls in catering. 'Take care, Jeremy. Speak to you soon.' Everything seems in order, so having eliminated any doubts in this quarter, I turn my attention to AFSL, our handling agent.

Reaching its Control Room is no easy task. Terminal 2 is one of the oldest buildings at Heathrow and has been undergoing massive redevelopment to bring it in line with the remainder of the airport. While the improvements are obvious, trying to remember how to get to certain parts of the terminal can tax the sharpest of minds. As the developments have progressed, the builders have had to block off certain areas while opening up new ones, and it really has been a bit of a nightmare. After one particular week away from the place, I can remember returning to such an alien environment that I considered contacting a cartographer to assist me in my plight. Today, however, my luck is in – the obstacles appear to be the same as yesterday. What a relief!

Heading for the Control Room, I pass behind the check-in desks and bid everyone a jolly morning. I like to think that my cheerful attitude will rub off on everyone around me. I can't imagine how we'd survive if at least some of us did not smile some of the time. 'Bon morning all! It's a bit crowded in here, isn't it? I don't want to hear any tales about us being short-staffed later on!'

The staff are tightly squashed into a small room, which is of similar dimensions to the average domestic broom cupboard. 'Morning, what can we do for you?' asks one of the lucky ones who has found sanctuary behind a desk. 'Could you possibly make sure we write the boarding gate number on the boarding cards straight away, please? The aircraft is on Echo 40.'

By now, you are probably beginning to think that I have a hang-up about Echo 40. Well, you're quite right! Boarding gate 40 is located in a part of the airport known as the Europier, which was specially constructed to serve flights operating (surprise-surprise!) to Europe from both Terminals 1 and 2. The pier – the corridor along which the flight departure gates are situated – is adjacent to Terminal 1 (which is fair enough, given that most of the flights are processed through Terminal 1), but it means that it's a long walk from us in Terminal 2. So much so that some passengers can take anything up to twenty-five minutes to make it from Passport Control to the gate.

It's the need to eliminate the possibility of delay and ensure that the passengers arrive in time for the flight's departure that makes me so paranoid about this particular parking stand. Normally, for security reasons, we do not show the number of the departure gate until the staff are there to handle passengers, but, luckily for us, Gate 40 is in an area with shops, so passengers can wander around freely without posing any threat to security.

Heather, the AFSL agent, agrees to update the computer with the necessary information. 'Cheers, Heather. The staff can reach me in the office if there are any problems at check-in.'

Having successfully navigated my way through the construction site back to the office, I find that Gabi, our Passenger Services Agent (lovingly known as Gabichka), the second of our Polish contingent,

✈ Has somebody forgotten to tell me about a lightning strike, or is it a case of the Marie Celeste syndrome? This is the Europier area between Terminals 1 and 2, where travellers can do a spot of last-minute shopping before their flights. It isn't normally so quiet, but then again, it is early in the morning.

has arrived for her daily dose of fun. 'Greetings, Gabichka! How's things?' Busily tucking into an almond croissant, for which she seems to have a particular penchant, she raises her head and informs me that all is well.

Not wanting to disturb her breakfast, I go over to the printer to read the incoming telex messages. Our second flight, which is expected to arrive at 12.10, is just being loaded in Moscow, and I am eager to see the inbound passenger manifest as I am expecting a close friend to be on board. 'Gabs, I'm off to the gate shortly. Could you let me know when the inbound list comes through? I want to check that passenger Levina is on board.' 'No probs,' replies Gabi, having finished her tasty-looking croissant.

Not wanting to over-exert myself so early in the day, and in a bid to save some time, I drive over to Gate 40. It's now one hour and ten minutes before the

doors need to close and the crew are already on board. On the flight deck the captain and the first officer are busy going through the routine of checking the aircraft's systems. I do not like disturbing them while they are running through these all-important tasks, so I speak instead to the cabin crew to make sure they're happy with everything.

'How did you all sleep last night?' For some reason I always ask this question and always dread the reply. After all, even we hear the rumours about what the crews get up to in strange hotels! 'Okay, thanks,' comes the reassuring reply from the Chief Stewardess, who is extremely business-like, and knows her job very well. If there is a hair out of place, this stewardess will spot it. 'Has catering arrived yet?' I ask hesitantly. 'Yes. They are unloading all the equipment at the moment,' states the Chief Stewardess with a chill in her voice. She's really a pleasant person, but first thing in the morning when there's work to be done, she feels we can dispense with the pleasantries. Fair enough. My departing question, 'Have the English-language newspapers been delivered yet?' is met with an equally frosty response, 'I have them.' Leaving the aircraft in more than capable hands, I head towards the dreaded entrance of Gate 40.

'Jeremy – from Gabi,' hisses my radio. 'Go ahead, Gabichka.' 'Do you know anything about a Peruvian deportee going on the first flight?' 'No, sorry, I don't.' 'Well, Immigration have just been on the phone to confirm that they're intending to remove a Peruvian woman first thing.'

Dealing with persons who are no longer permitted entry to the United Kingdom (known to us as deportees) is often quite stressful. There are a number of factors that can result in a person being asked to leave, including arriving in Britain without a visa. As an airline, we are obliged under current legislation to ensure that the passengers we carry are in possession of valid entry documents. If passengers are found not to hold a valid entry visa on arrival, we are held responsible, fined and instructed to return them to their country of origin.

Before going through the entrance to the gate, I decide to call Gabi back to find out a few more details about the case. I may, for example, need to provide the passenger with a ticket at our expense. Sure enough, the lady in question arrived in 1993 from Lima, having travelled via Moscow with Aeroflot, and has no ticket to travel.

'Jeremy, Immigration are going to escort the passenger to the gate, so I'll get the ticket sent out to you.' Thanking Gabi, I swipe my security pass through a special reader and, like a scene from Ali Baba, the doors unlock automatically.

Entering the heart of the Europier, I see my boarding staff team hard at it – gathering up passengers, of course! The team, headed up by Marie-Claude (another super-efficient female airline worker, who, unlike my colleague on the aircraft, loves to chat) are making tremendous efforts to achieve the desired on-time departure.

'Marie-Claude – morning, love. No need to ask how you are. I can see you're on top form.' 'Naturally, darling,' comes the reply from this sophisticated French woman. 'Has anyone advised you about the deportee?' I ask the team. With an air of authority, Marie-Claude replies in the affirmative. This is good news. It is possible that I will not be at the gate when the passenger arrives and it is important that the woman's travel documents are handed directly to the crew for safe keeping throughout the journey. People destroying their passports during a flight is not unheard of. The theory, presumably, is that if we cannot prove where they have originated from, it is more difficult for Immigration to deport them and they might then be able to stay in the country.

The feeling of tranquillity is suddenly broken by the sight of the Chief Stewardess heading along the corridor. As she struts towards us, she has a look in her eye and a shine on her boots that reminds me of Colonel Kleb of James

Bond fame. 'Are you all right?' asks Marie-Claude. 'Well, I was, but I have this awful feeling things are about to change,' I reply. The Colonel then informs me that catering have left her no bread rolls. Now, for anyone who has ever flown I'm sure there's no need to explain that bread rolls can often be the highlight of in-flight meals, especially if they are pre-heated as our rolls generally are. 'I'll get on to them immediately,' I reply, 'although I'm not sure how quickly they can get any rolls out to us.' The Chief Stewardess, while not happy at having no rolls, knows me and is confident I will sort the problem out.

After several attempts, I manage to get through to catering. 'Hi! It's Jeremy here at Aeroflot. We seem to be missing our bread rolls.' I'm half expecting the guy at the other end of the phone to quip that that's not all we're missing and am surprised to hear him say instead: 'Oh, that's strange. I could have sworn we loaded them on to the truck with the ice.' This may well have been the case, but I'm not about to accuse any of my colleagues of being blind. I want to live to see my friend arrive later in the day.

'We'll try getting some out to you now.' The word 'try' is *very* worrying in such circumstances. I have no bread rolls and, whatever the reason may be for this, I need them as quickly as possible. So someone telling me they are going to 'try' is not really what I want to hear.

'Marie-Claude,' I gulp, 'there may be a slight delay. We are going to have to wait for catering to bring us some bread rolls. I don't suppose for a minute that one of our passengers will have been to a baker's on their way to the gate.' Trying not to let the thought of a delay show on her face, Marie-Claude smiles grimly. 'I know,' I say to cheer her up, 'maybe I could ask some of the Russian passengers if they have packed some sandwiches. It's not uncommon for Russians to be that well-organized. I speak from experience. My friend, for example, who I'm expecting today, never lets me leave for the airport without a packed lunch.' By this time, Marie-Claude and the staff are convinced of my insanity as I chunter on about where I might find a baker's dozen.

Just as I strike on the idea of raiding a catering truck as it passes us by, I spot the Immigration escorts in the distance, leading a woman in her early forties who's weighed down by a mountain of baggage. The sight of the escorts lifts my spirits, even though there is clearly going to be an excess baggage situation. At least the deportee is accompanied. I can still vividly remember the day when a Mongolian deportee checked in, collected his travel documents from Immigration staff, then upped and disappeared. I had a team of scouts hunting high and low for him, but to this day we do not know where he vanished to. My suspicions about Heathrow being the Twilight Zone were reaffirmed by this mysterious occurrence. However, with escorts on the ground today, there is obviously not going to be a repeat of that incident. Nevertheless, on seeing the full extent of the passenger's baggage, I begin to wish I really was in the equivalent of the Bermuda Triangle.

While we, as an airline, might be required by the Government to remove deportees, we are not obliged to carry limitless quantities of their luggage for free. However, acutely aware of the sensitivity of such circumstances, I'm always prepared to bend a little to help people out. On this occasion I'm not entirely sure, though, what assistance I can offer. The Peruvian passenger has been allowed to come to the gate with six enormous suitcases that remind me of those double-door fridges you find in America and some posh UK stores.

If the passenger is able to pay excess baggage charges, there won't be a problem. However, I very much doubt that this lady is going to be in a position to pay approximately £22.00 per kilo (this being the charge for 1kg of excess baggage from London to Lima).

'Sorry guys, but why has this passenger been allowed to come to the gate with so much baggage?' I ask the escorts. My curiosity has got the better of me and I'm hoping they can explain what has happened. 'Sorry, but that's what she had with her when we collected her this morning,' comes the somewhat vexed response from one of the escorts.

Knowing it is not really their concern, I turn my attention to the distressed Peruvian. 'Good morning, madam. Did anyone explain to you that you will have to pay something for your baggage?' Silence.

✈ Hand baggage always poses a problem: some people think that if they can carry it, it counts as being acceptable to take into the cabin. The parcel here nearly slipped past me, as I'm explaining to the AFSL ramp team leader. However, it was just a wee bit too big to be concealed by the offending passenger.

This is a first – normally people throw themselves on your mercy. I begin to get the feeling that this lady doesn't speak any English. 'Sorry, madam, do you understand?' The next silence is interrupted by Gabi on the radio. 'Jeremy, passenger Levina is on board the SU241.' 'That's great, Gabi,' I quickly reply, wanting to return to the matter in hand. 'Could you phone catering for me and see where they are with my bread rolls? Cheers, hon.' I turn to the Peruvian deportee, who, by now, is crying. It transpires that the lady speaks only Spanish – not a language I'm fully familiar with.

 Imagine the scene: I am just ten minutes from needing to close the door of the aircraft, I have Colonel Kleb's equivalent on board breathing fire about her non-existent bread rolls, a Peruvian deportee who has enough baggage to employ a train of Sherpas, and on top of everything else there are still twenty-seven passengers missing.

Needing to push things along a little, I say, 'Marie-Claude, don't worry about the baggage here, I'll deal with that. Can you ask one of the boarders to head off down the pier to look for the missing passengers.' 'Someone is already on their way there,' she replies in her ever-efficient manner. Good, at least that's something.

As the calm begins to dissolve around me, I can see Boris Eremin, our Station Manager, speaking to the Peruvian deportee. Boris is very talented with languages, but I had no idea he could also survive in Spanish. I am very grateful when he manages to explain the baggage situation to our distressed passenger. 'Mr Eremin,' I interrupt, 'can I leave things in your capable hands? I'm just going down on to the stand to see if I can grab a truck with some bread rolls.' Running (which I only ever do in extreme circumstances), I can see a truck on the stand next to us. Catching the attention of the driver, I yell: 'Any chance I can pinch a few bread rolls, mate?'

Because we are a friendly bunch at Heathrow and, contrary to popular belief, we like to help one another as much as possible, I am confident that the truck-driver will be able to come to my rescue. 'Sure. How many do you need?' With a slight gulp, I coolly answer:

'Oh, about 300, if poss.' Convinced I have pushed my luck, I am pleasantly surprised to find that the driver is more than willing to meet my needs.

Thank God, there are just five minutes before departure and the bread crisis is solved. As I hand the booty over to the stewardess, she says, 'Excellent. Now ... how many passengers are missing?' Phew! I've hardly got my breath back. I told you she was business-like, didn't I?

More running, this time back to the boarding-gate team to see how we are doing. Success, the deportee has paid a small amount towards her baggage charges – leaving me with no choice but to waive the remainder – and has already taken her seat on board the aircraft. My first major challenges of the day have been resolved and I'm left wondering what next? 'Jeremy, you won't want to hear this, but we are still three passengers missing,' states Marie-Claude in a matter-of-fact tone. 'Oh? Why am I not surprised by that?'

Missing passengers are definitely the curse of every airline. For the life of me, I cannot understand why it is that 176 passengers can make it in time for the departure, while the remaining three are utterly incapable. 'Have we checked the shops and VAT reclaim?', I ask, sounding no less matter of fact. 'Yes. One of the girls is just heading back from there, and is still looking to see if she can spot the missing three.'

Just as I go to instruct the baggage-handlers to search for and unload the missing passengers' luggage (no aircraft, for security reasons, is allowed to depart with baggage belonging to a passenger who has checked in, but failed to show at the departure gate), I hear a rather out-of-breath staff member shouting down the radio that she has located the happy wanderers.

'Where are you at the moment?' I ask. This may seem a silly question, but knowing their precise location enables me to gauge how long it will be before we have our full complement and are ready to depart: fairly shortly, Air Traffic Control will need to be informed about our state of readiness. 'We'll be with you in a couple of minutes. I found the passengers heading towards Terminal 1.' I am in no way astonished by this revelation. I have even seen staff go the wrong way when they reach the Europier, so blaming the passengers for holding up everyone else is simply not on.

Finally, just thirteen minutes behind schedule, the aircraft receives clearance from Air Traffic Control to push back from the stand for take-off and make its way to Moscow. I can now return to the office with the satisfaction of having kept our toughest stewardess at bay for another day.

 'Do you guys want a lift back to the terminal, or are you all eager for some exercise?' Without any hesitation, the boarding-gate team beat me back to the car for the five-minute drive to the office.

Leaving Marie-Claude and the others heading for breakfast at McDonalds, I pass the airline desks in the departure hall. If you are ever passing through Terminal 2 and you see staff manning the desks, it can mean only one thing – trouble. Why? Because the desks are manned only when there is a flight delay! And right now two of AFSL's staff are behind the desks looking rather dejected. 'Morning folks!' I greet them. 'What's up?' 'There's a delay on the Syrian,' comes the melancholy answer from a rather careworn-looking Ms Brown. 'Cheer up, love,' I reply, 'at least Syrian passengers tend to speak English. You could be sat there trying to deal with a plane-load of my punters, and you did say only yesterday that your Russian is rusty.'

Ms Brown manages a smile and we chat about the delay. It appears that our colleagues at Syrian Arab Airlines have a technical delay with their aircraft, which is now receiving the attention of British Airways engineers. We have all experienced this kind of problem in the past, and will inevitably do so again in the future. The strange thing is that when you do have a technical delay, you always feel as though you are the only people in the world who have to cope with such a trauma. I bid Ms Brown and her colleague farewell, hoping that the problem will be rectified before the passengers start to adopt a rabid look.

Not wanting to tempt fate too often, I elect to return to the office via the baggage hall, which, although out of my way, dispenses with the need for me to pass through the Tardis. It also gives me the chance to catch up with the staff in the Baggage Services Department, who are, without doubt, the unsung heroes of the airline industry. Every

✈ 'Excuse me, guv, don't I know you?' is often the quip that colleagues around the airport use to greet me. However, this is a brief encounter with my colleague Andy from Aeroflot's Cargo department, who is also waiting for the arrival of our Ilyushin IL86. 'I hope they don't send it off to Echo 47; I don't think I've got enough petrol!'.

day they ceaselessly try to reunite passengers with their missing luggage. Bags go missing for a whole host of reasons, not least because they are incorrectly labelled at check-in, but they are usually located within forty-eight hours of going AWOL. This reassuring thought, however, is not much comfort to the staff while they are battling to calm the nerves of naturally distressed passengers.

I enter the hall expecting to find a queue of passengers raising mayhem and demanding to know why staff are incapable of employing extra sensory perception to locate missing items, but am pleasantly surprised to see the hall is all but deserted. 'What's up? Where are they all this morning?' I ask, feeling a bit like a military leader wanting to know where the enemy has got to. 'I know ...' I exclaim skittishly, 'they're trying to lull you into a false sense of security!'

Brenda, a long-suffering agent of the baggage hall, glances over the top of her glasses and informs me: 'You should have been here an hour ago. We had more than twenty of 'em without bags.' Twenty passengers may seem an insignificant number to you, but, believe me, it isn't! Dealing with just one passenger who has lost their luggage can be traumatic enough, but twenty … well, that can be suicidal.

Only too aware of the stress my colleagues are under in this all-but-forgotten section of the terminal, and not wanting to upset them by making them recount the traumas of their morning, I enquire: 'Have you got much for us at the moment, folks?' 'No,' replies Brenda, reaching for her coffee cup with its all-important caffeine boost. 'We seem to be pretty clear of your bags at present, Jeremy. There's just that one bag of dried fish and dates from Friday. We're hoping to reach its owner later on today.' 'That must be really smelly by now, surely to God?' I say, but I'm not in the least surprised any more by what some people choose to put in their luggage. 'Yeah, we'll probably have to dispose of the fish tomorrow if we can't reach the owner,' states Brenda, who has seen it all before.

Leaving them surrounded by the aroma of decaying fish to do battle with the latest arrivals from around Europe, I head for the office.

 Arriving back at the nerve centre, as it is lovingly known, I discover Gabichka deep in conversation with Kashinka. (I appreciate there are too many names ending in 'ka' in this book, but you can thank the Russians for having a system whereby people's first names are put into a diminutive form when addressed by close friends.) Not wanting to interrupt their discussion, I make myself a cuppa and sit at my desk looking at the various piles of paper. It's no good – if I'm ever again to have a clear desk, I must start to make inroads to my paper mountain.

✈ 'Excuse me, sir. Are you who I think you are? … Mmm, I thought so. I saw your mugshot on a wanted poster back at the nick. You do realize that the sign means NO ENTRY, even for you?' I always try to find time to chat with Richard, one of the beat bobbies at the airport, whose job it is to protect and police Heathrow. You just never know when you might need a policeman around here.

'Girls,' I grimace, 'I'm sorry to interrupt, but I'd like to try and clear some of this rubbish off my desk today. If you don't mind too much, I'll leave you two to deal with the second flight. I want to go out and meet the arrival anyway because Natasha is coming today.' Kashinka, who looks as stunning as always, interrupts her conversation and says, 'If you want to get on with your paperwork, Jeremy, be our guest. We're going down to check-in shortly anyway.'

You must understand that I don't really want to sit and do any paperwork, but needs must, and it does give me an opportunity to escape the trials and tribulations of life in the terminal. Plumping for the largest pile of letters, I come across correspondence from Her Majesty's Immigration Service. Is there no escaping the grip of Big Brother today? What with the Peruvian saga earlier this morning, I'm beginning to get the impression that someone at Immigration has got it in for me. The letter informs me of the decision, by the Chief Immigration Officer, to uphold a fine levied against us in relation to an Afghan couple who had arrived earlier in the year without travel documents.

This particular couple (according to information received from my colleagues) had boarded our aircraft in Moscow with Pakistani passports, which they subsequently destroyed by cutting them up and flushing them down the toilet during the flight to London. As I said earlier, the theory seems to be that if they have no documents on arrival we cannot prove where they have originated from and it is more difficult for Immigration to deport them.

Destroying documents, however, can be a very risky business, as one passenger who arrived at Moscow's Sheremetyevo Airport approximately four years ago discovered. He's still there. No, not living in Moscow – living in the airport! His home is now the departure lounge because to date he has refused to say where he is from and the authorities have been unable to deport him. Although they have their suspicions, they have been unable to prove his nationality. This man is not unique. There is the famous case of a stateless national (as they are known) living in a Paris airport for years. So famous has he become that a film has been made about his life.

Looking at the letter, I decide that making further appeals to the Immigration Service in Croydon will not result in a reversal of its decision. Immigration staff working in the terminal had weakened any case we might have had by quickly establishing the couple's true nationality. There was also little scope for us to appeal on the basis that, as far as we were concerned, the couple had left Moscow fully documented with passports. And even if I had had copies of the passports the passengers had disposed of on the plane, they were probably forged, so a fine would have been inevitable anyway. Did I not say that someone out there had got it in for me!

I'm not going to let the thought of a £4000 fine from the Government upset me so early in the day – and help, in the form of displacement therapy, is at hand. A passenger has written a letter to thank us all. Her parents had been involved in a serious car accident in Karachi and we had managed to get her a seat on an already over-booked flight so that she could be with them in the hospital. I am delighted to read that all is now well and that her parents are both on the mend. It's rare for people to write letters of thanks nowadays. But not so rare for them to write letters of complaint! Whenever we see a letter of thanks, it lifts our spirits, and, for an all too brief moment, makes us feel as though it is worth putting up with all the problems we encounter.

The peace and tranquillity of the empty office is broken by the sound of Gabi's voice over the radio. 'Base – from Gabi. Any sign of the aircraft yet?'  Startled, I look up from my computer at the clock. It's 11.50 already! 'Stand by, Gabs, I'll have a look at BASIS for you.' BASIS is the airport's own computerized information system from which we are able to see details of all arriving and departing aircraft, as well as more general data about such things as the weather. Trying not to sound as though I have been in a world of my own, I inform Gabi that the aircraft's in the zone for Echo 9.

Grabbing my radio, I head off down the corridor towards W.H. Smith. W.H. Smith? Yes, I know this may seem strange – our aircraft is about to land and right now I appear to be more interested in checking out the local newsagent. But, no, I've not taken leave of my senses, or developed a sudden interest in passenger shopping habits. I urgently need to buy some flowers for my friend, Natasha. The giving of flowers in Russia is a great tradition and I do not want to fail my heritage by not presenting a close friend with a floral tribute.

'Have you got any flowers today?' I enquire anxiously of the girl behind the till. 'Not here, but the shop next to arrivals has got some.' Yes – but it's the other end of the terminal! The other end of the terminal! I've got about five minutes to buy the flowers, go through the Central Staff Search area and then run along the concourse to Gate 9.

Why, I hear you ask, do I need to run, especially if my friend knows that I will arrive at the aircraft anyway? Well, if you had met Natasha, you would know why I need to make sure I am at the aircraft as she comes off. Firstly, she is old enough to be my mother, which, in my book, is enough to demand respect. Secondly, Natasha is a senior member of the staff at Moscow University, teaching English. Now, anyone who has ever met a Russian teacher will confirm that they have a certain manner about them, which renders all but the Herculean among us intimidated. When they say, 'Do your homework,' by God you do it, and it is therefore difficult for them to make any requests outside their working environment sound like anything other than a demand. For all of this, Natasha is one of the kindest people I have ever met and a real delight to spend time with. Indeed, I tend to stay with her and her family whenever I am in Moscow, and often go out to their *dacha* (country cottage) at the weekends to relax.

'Mr Eremin, is the aircraft on the stand yet?' comes my rather out-of-breath question over the radio. 'Yes, Jeremy. The aircraft has just arrived.' It's an unforgivable five months since I last saw Natasha, so with the thought of having to eat humble pie for the remainder of the day if I don't get there on time, I decide to impersonate someone of athletic build by running as fast as possible. The scene clearly creates a flurry of interest among my friends on the concourse, as they immediately begin shouting at me, wanting to know where I have

✈ Natasha's looking resplendent in her freshly applied lipstick for the camera (much to my amusement). This is her flat in Moscow, where she entertained me and three foreign exchange students one evening, providing them with their first experience of traditional Russian fare, not to mention hospitality.

dropped my five pound note. 'What are you like, you lot?', I utter as I pass them.

My efforts have paid off. Collapsing at the end of the gate, I catch a glimpse of Natasha heading towards me. '*Privyet dorogoi droog moi,*' comes the commanding voice of this Great Russian Bear, as she heads towards me with arms open. Greeting Natasha with her flowers, '*Privyet, Natash. Kak ty doletela?*' – and, wanting to know how hard the cabin crew have been working, I ask what kind of journey she has had. Everything was fine, she informs me, although she would have liked a few more cups of tea – five having failed to quench her killer thirst!

I now face the ultimate challenge. Yes, even for me, trying to get a word in edgeways with Natasha is nigh on impossible. She really can talk the hind legs off a donkey, so I listen patiently as we head for Immigration. Not surprisingly, there is a long queue of non-EU (European Union) citizens waiting to have their documents checked.

'Jeremy, where are you?' comes the voice of the Tsaritsa through the radio. Wrestling with my friend's hand baggage, I manage to push the button on my radio and reply, 'I'm at Passport Control, Kashinka. Why? Have you got a problem down there?' 'Well, there's a passenger at Central Search with a knife,' Kasia informs me, 'and they need one of us to go and translate. I wondered if it would be poss for you to go?'

Reluctant to leave Natasha to expire in the queue, I ask Kasia whether she is able to go. But, unfortunately, both she and Gabi are knee-deep in excess baggage problems, so Natasha insists I leave her to make her own way to our office. 'Are you sure, Natasha? At least, let me take you to the front of the queue.' Sorry everyone, this is one of those rare occasions when I take advantage of being a staff member and pull rank – wouldn't you?

 Leaving my bear-like friend at the head of the snake of people, I make my way through the baggage hall and along the corridor back into the departure lounge. As I approach Passenger Central Search (the security point prior to Passport Control in the departures area), I can see an elderly man being questioned by the police. Correction, the police appear to be asking lots of questions and getting no answers. It's not that the passenger is trying to land himself a role in the latest episode of *The Bill*, you understand, by being a hard case and refusing to snitch on his accomplices. No, he simply doesn't understand a word of what's being said to him.

He also has no idea that, unlike in Russia where eight-inch military-style knives are commonly used by people around the house, in the garden, etc., it's a criminal offence in Britain to be in possession of such a lethal-looking object. Now I am faced with the prospect of explaining that his knife will be confiscated by the police and that although he is on the verge of departing from London back to Moscow, he may face arrest.

'Hi, guys! Is it the usual with a knife?' I greet them, knowing full well what the response will be. 'Yes. Could you just ask him what he uses it for, please?' requests one of the terminal's regular beat bobbies. It comes as no surprise when the passenger informs me that the knife has been in his possession for twenty-three years and has been used for everything from whittling wood to cutting up sausages. 'Sorry, lads,' I say, 'it's the usual.' 'Okay, well we're going to have to take the knife and, as you know, we are obliged to arrest the passenger. Could you inform him of the procedures?'

As I explain the situation to the passenger, he stands looking at me in utter amazement, and who can blame him? This foreign travel lark can be a really confusing experience, can it not? The passenger is led off to Heathrow's police station, leaving me to retrieve his baggage and await details from the police about when he will be released. The process normally takes about three hours, so, needless to say, he will miss the flight departing at 13.30 and be forced to return to Moscow tomorrow lunchtime.

'Kasia, the passenger's been arrested. I've already advised the COP [remember that famous code of ours for the Control Room] to off-load the passenger from the flight, and I'll go down to baggage and arrange for his luggage to be held over until tomorrow.' Hearing the news, Kasia asks: 'Was the passenger travelling alone?' 'Fortunately,' I reply, 'he is. I've got the telephone number of his wife, so when I get back to the office, I'll call her and let her know what's happening.'

Making my way along the warren of corridors back to the office, I can hear the banter of Gabichka and the Tsaritsa over the radio. With the exception of the man with the dagger, things seem to have sorted themselves out and the girls are looking forward to an on-time departure. I know this is where I'm supposed to feel jealous and sick at the thought that they've managed to get everything to come together in time for the magical departure at 13.30 without me, but I'm not. I'm simply relieved that another flight is going to get back into the air more or less on schedule. It goes without saying really that unless an aircraft is in the air, it is not really earning its keep!

✈ Me with Harry. When not working at Aeroflot, he has been known to stand in for Lionel Jeffries, opening the odd village fête...

Recalling the tropical temperatures in the office first thing, I open the door with some trepidation, half-expecting to find Natasha on the floor, having passed out from the heat. Silly me! She has the constitution of a bear and is already busy in the kitchen preparing tea for everyone. Our desks are awash with Russian chocolates, cakes and biscuits. Bang goes that elusive diet I keep promising myself. Harry, another of the long-suffering Aeroflot staff who, by the way, doesn't speak Russian, is delighted to be able to engage Natasha in conversation about life in the motherland. Our Polish contingent has returned and everyone seems to be intent on devouring all the food they can see. Knowing that I am going to have the pleasure of taking Natasha back to Colchester with me, where she will be teaching Russian to English students at the local university, I decide to leave the jollities and return to my paperwork for a couple of hours.

As I struggle up the steps to the car park with my friend's baggage (because the lifts are under repair), it dawns on me that car park lifts everywhere are  nearly always under repair. It is all too easy, I reflect, to pack far too much – and that thought makes me even more resolute about excess baggage problems. Shame, I know!

'Natash! What on earth have you got in here? These bags weigh a ton!' Natasha, trying really hard not to imply that being a mere man I represent the weaker sex, simply states in her deep, bear-like tone, '*Zaichik*, I've got lots of books, newspapers, magazines and some Russian tea, of course. Oh, not to mention packets of those lovely little Russian alphabet biscuits – you know, the ones I use for my beginner classes.' Thoughts of needing surgery for a hernia pass through my mind as I put my friend's four large bags into the car, which, incidentally, is parked on the fourth floor!

For the first time in months, my journey home seems to whiz by as I listen to all Natasha's news from Moscow. Believe it or not, I'm actually enjoying not having to say too much for a change. And I just sit back in that all too familiar auto-pilot mode that guides me home to Colchester.

CHAPTER 3

IT'S A DOG'S LIFE

SILENCE ENGULFS ME as I make my weary way to work without Natasha alongside me in the passenger seat. I am faced with the prospect of sharing my day with the BBC team, who are planning to film some more material for their fly-on-the-wall TV documentary, *Airport*. As I drive along, it dawns on me that I could so easily have ended up appearing in the TV series *Hotel*. When I left school at sixteen, I went along to see my Careers Advisor in the hope that, between us, we might hit upon some divine inspiration and manage to find a path into my chosen career. (Actually, 'went along' is not, strictly speaking, true. I was, in fact, forced to go along by the Department of Employment.)

Being young and incredibly foolish (I know, some things never change), I listened patiently to the advice I was given and vaguely remember being told, 'The airline industry is very difficult to break into, especially if you live more than a hundred miles from a major airport! Perhaps you should consider a temporary move into hotels and catering, where you could gain valuable people skills, etc., which may then lead to a career in the airline industry. At least there are hotels in your local area!'

← No, I'm not moonlighting on the *Encyclopaedia Britannica* stand, I'm helping an Armenian passenger fathom out how to re-claim her VAT from HM Government.

Sure enough, I fell for it. After all, I did live a fair distance from Heathrow, and at the time the only thing I could drive was my mum round the bend! I wrote letter after letter, in fact almost 250 letters, to hotels and received only a handful of replies (all negative), which I know is nothing extraordinary nowadays. Feeling very dejected, I sat at home wondering if I would ever find a job, let alone one which might help me into the airline industry.

Then my luck changed, or so I thought, when I received a call from a five-star hotel in Surrey. 'Is that Jeremy Spake?' asked an authoritative-sounding female voice down the line. 'Er, yes it is,' I replied, thinking that it was the She-Devil from the Department of Employment, whom I had met several weeks earlier. 'Good. I'm the Housekeeping Manager and have just read your letter. We have a vacancy for a junior in the Housekeeping Department and would like you to come for interview tomorrow at 10 a.m.' It was all so matter of fact that I was left feeling somewhat shell-shocked.

Not wanting to miss the opportunity, I duly persuaded my dad to give me a lift to Surrey. (Fathers really do make very good taxi-drivers, don't they?) Arriving at the hotel, I was met by what appeared to be the real-life equivalent of Hyacinth Bucket in *Keeping Up Appearances*. My first impression was of a dour, business-like housekeeper, who was clearly determined to maintain the status of this five-star property.

These illusions were soon shattered when I was asked a number of leading questions about my personal habits. 'Do you smoke?' 'Are you into drugs?' 'Do you drink heavily?' 'Are you involved in anything remotely debauched?' Being only sixteen, I was somewhat shocked – and confused – by this line of questioning. 'No, not really,' I replied cautiously, 'I might have an occasional glass of wine.' I was stunned to hear her say: 'You're a boring little git, aren't you?'

The interview ended shortly afterwards and I was left wondering what kind of people skills I might have learned at this five-star den of iniquity. The disappointed woman had the affront to call me the next day and offer me the job. No thanks, I thought, give me airlines any day.

Driving along, I catch a glimpse of the rotating radar of Heathrow and I am more than grateful that my day with the BBC will be spent at the airport and not in some hotel. The Beeb's film crew does add to my daily pressures, but we have an understanding that they will give me space to work and not get under my feet. Today's crew of three – producer, cameraman and sound technician – are a friendly bunch, so I'm looking forward to an enjoyable day, even though this is only Day Three of seven.

Do you ever get the feeling that someone's got it in for you? Well, this morning I was convinced from the moment I entered the office that somebody some-  where is definitely trying to do away with me. It can only be sabotage. The air conditioning has been working overtime and the temperature is now reminiscent of winter in Siberia. Reaching for my trusty fur hat in a bid to stave off hypothermia from a temperature of minus twenty degrees centigrade, I am delighted to hear the dulcet tones of my colleague, Igor, from the other side of the door.

Igor (Gorskii as he is known to me) is our Station Engineer and some might argue that he came from the same mould as yours truly. And, difficult as it is for me to admit this, on account of our being such good friends, he does bear a remarkable resemblance to Stalin. He is also without doubt – hard though this may be to believe – as mad as I am, and that is what makes working with him such a pleasure. My family is still trying to recover from the shock that there is somebody else just like me on the planet! Anyway, Igor's been away for two weeks on holiday and I hadn't realized until I saw him again just how much I'd missed his humour around the place. One thing's for certain – the rest of the office will be reaching for their ear-plugs now that he's back! He really is an exuberant, lively, fun-loving person who always manages to stir things up.

Igor is no more conventional in his greetings than he is in his general behaviour, so I'm not in least surprised when he turns and says, 'Jemskii, you snake, look what I've found in the corridor – one of those KGB infiltration groups pretending to be a BBC film crew!' (Trying to explain why Igor calls me a snake would take far too long. You'll have to take my word that it's got nothing whatsoever to do with me being

ВЫХО

reptilian.) 'Behave yourself, Gorskii,' I retort. 'They're not from the KGB – look at all the Japanese camera equipment – only Americans can afford to be that flash. They must be from the CIA.' On that note, I usher Igor and the film crew into the Siberian atmosphere.

Having already tried to warm my hands on the spluttering coffee-maker, I know there's sufficient to give everyone a nice cuppa to start the day. Igor, who seems determined to assist the Ministers of Europe by putting enough sugar into his cup to halve any sugar-mountain that may exist, begins to share his holiday experiences with Sarichka, the producer from the Beeb. (As you may have guessed, we've changed her name from the English Sarah to the Russian Sarichka. She does actually speak Russian, so that seems fair enough.) Not wanting to interrupt Igor in mid-flow, I decide to get on with the daily battle plan and head for the computer to generate our report.

As I make my way across the room, the phones begin to light up like a Christmas tree. If entering the Tardis is a lottery, then choosing which phone to answer is a bit like being a contestant on Bruce Forsyth's *Play Your Cards Right*. Going higher or lower up the row of flashing lines can mean the difference between a quiet morning and an instantaneous unpleasant sinking of the spirits. The need to choose the right phone, however, is immediately eliminated by the sight of Line One flashing. We, like world leaders, have a hot line to our main office in Central London, and yes, you've guessed, Line One is it. Normally, the only person to use this line is our General Manager, so I'm somewhat surprised to find Verna, the Reservations Supervisor, on the other end of the phone.

'Jeremy, we've just had a request from the Russian Embassy to book a stretcher case on Saturday's St Petersburg flight. Can I ask you to do the necessary and confirm all the details to us?' From experience, I know that dealing with medical cases (MEDA, as they are known to us) can be fraught with problems. MEDA cases have a nasty habit of becoming complicated and going wrong, and even with the

---

✦ 'What do you think of my new hairdo?'. This is Igor, my friend, colleague and technical adviser. He is always eager to please the General Secretary and knows that I will not take kindly to any technical defect that will result in the aircraft being delayed.

best-laid plans, you can never be certain you've covered every angle.

Occasionally, however, dealing with MEDA problems can bring a smile to the face. I recall a story told to me by Rita, a nurse working for British Airways at the airport. She took a phone call one evening from a lady making enquiries about how soon after a stroke her sister might be cleared for travel. 'Provided there have been no complications and a full medical recovery has been achieved,' Rita informed the caller, 'we would be happy to accept a passenger ten days after a stroke.' Then, being a true professional – and wanting to show concern – Rita asked, 'When did your sister suffer her stroke?' 'Oh, she hasn't had it yet,' the caller informed Rita. 'I'm psychic and I've had a premonition that she's going to suffer a stroke just before travelling to Australia. Thanks for the information, it's been most useful.' As the caller hung up, Rita was left wondering whether she'd just been involved in some strange Arthur C. Clarke paranormal experiment. But no, she was simply sitting at Heathrow in the Medical Centre, trying to get on with her job!

'Verna, what exactly is wrong with the passenger?' I ask, not really wanting to become too involved as, clearly, this is not going to be anywhere near as simple as Rita's call! 'He's been involved in a car accident and is reported to have broken his neck.' The word 'reported' worries me. It indicates that someone somewhere down the line is not certain what is wrong, and that spells trouble because in order for me to be able to organize everything efficiently, I need precise and accurate information. 'Which hospital is the passenger in at the moment?' I ask. 'I'll need to speak to his doctor so that I can provide St Petersburg with all the necessary medical details.'

Verna informs me that the Russian Embassy doctor has been liaising with the hospital and that he will provide me with all the information I need. (The patient comes from St Petersburg, but is employed by Russia's diplomatic service in Moscow.)

Like most airlines, Aeroflot has its own medical department which is responsible for assessing a passenger's condition and, where appropriate, authorizing travel arrangements. In order to assist the medical department with its assessment, it is necessary for me to send a telex with a full medical report from the local hospital. The patient's file is then read by our own doctors, who in turn consider the level of risk involved in transporting a medical passenger.

'Verna, does the embassy doctor really understand that he should ring me with the details?' I ask, not wanting to sound as perturbed as I feel by the prospect of a stretcher case on a Saturday, the second busiest day of the week for us. Saturday, I hasten to add, is Day Six of seven, and my energy by then will be shot to pieces. 'Sure. He's going to try and call you later today, or first thing in the morning,' Verna replies.

Knowing that I can send a telex to St Petersburg with the final details tomorrow, I decide to go ahead and enter the booking on the computer based on the initial information received. In a Tupolev TU154, the type of aircraft we are expecting to use for Saturday's flight, I will need to block off four Business Class seats for the stretcher to be fitted across, plus one seat for the nurse who will accompany the passenger. This done, I send a copy of the booking, with a brief outline of our requirements, to Verna and my colleagues in St Petersburg. Things, I reflect, will be very interesting on Saturday!

During this rather worrying telephone call, Kasia and Harry have arrived in the office and are listening to the latest revelations from Igor, who is already  enjoying his second cup of coffee. 'Jeremy, is it okay if we mike you up now?' asks Sarichka, who wants to start capturing the daily events on film. The sound technician then wires me up, which sounds more painful than it is! The cameraman starts up and the producer wades straight in by asking me to give a run-down of the day's anticipated events. Being asked to predict what might occur during a shift always makes me laugh. This is, after all, the Twilight Zone where anything can – and often does – happen!

'Today, we have just the one outward-bound flight from Heathrow, the SU242 destined for Moscow, at 13.30,' I begin. 'Looking at the daily report, it'll be a near-full flight with 181 passengers, of which forty-five are transiting in Moscow to other destinations. Most of the transit passengers are travelling to Calcutta, so there's going to be loads of haggling down at check-in. In addition, we have the SU582 flight arriving at 18.05 this evening from Tokyo, and our handling agents at Gatwick will also be busy dealing with one of our three flights a week arriving from St Petersburg at 13.25.'

I am interrupted by the Empress Kashinka, who, having applied a new layer of lipstick, is busy answering the phones. 'Jeremy, the police have just phoned to let us know that the elderly guy with the knife from yesterday will definitely be travelling today. I've booked him already. Have you still got his wife's number in Moscow?' Grateful that I have and that I will not need to implore forgiveness from my regal colleague, I answer in the affirmative.

'Be so kind [Kasia always says this when she wants you to do something for her] and phone her for me, Jeremy.' It's always a pleasure to help Kashinka, who, like Igor, is a kindred spirit. Phoning Moscow will be no problem, or so I think.

The *pensionerka* (the Russian word for female pensioner, and I make no apologies for it ending in 'ka' – you know the formula by now), is confused by her husband's arrest. Who wouldn't be under the circumstances? Convincing her that all is well, is not easy. This lady can remember the events of Stalin's purges and the introduction of gulags. After twenty challenging minutes, I seem to have succeeded in putting her mind at rest and she is now looking forward to seeing her husband just twenty-four hours later than she had expected him to arrive home.

Bidding the charming old lady farewell, I notice that time, as always, is against me. It's gone 10 a.m. already. Check-in will be starting in less than half an hour and I need to get my skates on if the BBC is going to be able to see check-in being set up. Is this, I hear you cry, the stuff that television is made of? Granted, such events are usually fairly nondescript, but when there's a television crew around, people have this habit of wanting to be seen. You know the kind of thing, I mean. You're sat watching the *Six O'Clock News* and there is nearly always some fool in the background shouting, 'Hello, Mum,' and leaping about all over the place and waving their arms.

This morning is no exception. As we are setting up the five desks required to process the 180 or so passengers, a gentleman approaches me wanting to haggle away 25 kilos of excess baggage. Clearly, he thinks that the camera is going to make me behave in a manner that is favourable to his plight. Silly man! As far as I'm concerned, the camera isn't there, so I have no intention of being any more lenient with him than I would be with anybody else.

Not wanting to launch into a great baggage debate so early in the check-in process, I inform the passenger that, 'I'm terribly sorry, sir, but at the moment we are not ready to open check-in. If you come back in a quarter of an hour, I'll be happy to discuss your baggage problems.' To this day, I have no idea why I always say I'll be 'happy' to discuss baggage because, if the truth be known, it is, for anyone who has worked at check-in for more than a day, one of the most boring topics in the world! Thanking me, the passenger turns very slowly away from me, making sure that the camera crew have plenty of time to pick up his beaming face.

Right on schedule, our four Economy Class desks and one First/Business Class desk, which is looking resplendent decked out with flowers and surrounded  by carpet, open for the daily grind. There are no prizes or Mensa certificates for guessing who is first in the queue. 'This very kind man said he would be happy to discuss my baggage problems, madam,' comes the soft tone of the passenger's voice as he tries to persuade the check-in agent that I'm about to waive all his excess charges, which come to around £400. He has not, however, banked on coming across Marina, another of our long-suffering check-in staff, who's very experienced in dealing with problems.

In her usual pleasant manner, she weighs the baggage and informs the passenger, 'You are actually 38 kilos over your allowance of 20, sir. I'll have a word with Mr Spake to see what – if anything – can be done to lower the charges.' Calling me over from the First Class desk, Marina shares the news with me. 'How many are travelling with the passenger, Marina?' I enquire. The answer will help me to establish exactly how many excess kilos the gentleman has. 'He's travelling alone,' replies Marina, who is already busy working out the excess charge on the computer.

'Please, sir,' says the now rather distressed-looking passenger more loudly, 'I'm requesting you consider my situation. I've been here for six months, you know, and am going home with many books. Can you do anything to help, please, sir?'

'We do have to charge you for some of this baggage, as I'm sure you're aware,' I explain. 'I'll allow you 30 kilos of checked-in baggage free (10 kilos more than he would be permitted normally), plus 8 kilos of hand baggage, but you will have to pay for the remaining 20 kilos.' As I finish telling him how much it will cost, his eyes begin to bulge and it is evident that any illusion he had about the camera waving a magic wand for him and his baggage have been shattered. He turns to tell the camera crew what a terrible man I am.

Over the years, in a bid to soften me up, every excess-baggage passenger either reminds me how many years they have been travelling with Aeroflot, or insists that British Airways would not expect them to pay. Knowing that British Airways is equally tough on excess baggage, I tend to ignore this type of remark. Today's passenger, having got his derogatory comments off his chest, decides to return to check-in to ask me to reconsider. This always brings a smile to my face. The passenger has just derided my character – this time in front of a BBC film crew – and now wants my sympathy! Resolute in my duty, I insist that he should either pay the charges outlined or leave some of his baggage behind. Sadly, the usual pendulum of abuse/pleasantry begins to swing to and fro, then after about fifteen minutes of this, the passenger relents and withdraws £400 in crisp £50 notes from his wallet.

Sarichka is intrigued by all these goings-on. So much so that she asks, 'Is that fairly typical behaviour from a passenger with too much baggage?' Resisting the temptation to laugh out loud, I respond, 'To be brutally honest, Sarichka, I'm surprised it took him so long to start calling me all the names under the sun. He's obviously still perfecting the art of how to be rude to airline employees. You only need to watch

✈ The labelling of luggage is extremely important. Once it leaves the check-in desks via the conveyer belt, it enters the 'catacombs', where it is loaded on to the correct flight... Well, that's the theory!

for an hour or so to see that this kind of behaviour is typical. It can be even worse when you've got a group of passengers with baggage problems, as they tend to gang together and become very aggressive. More often than not, they will also threaten you with physical abuse.' Thankfully, though, things appear to be under control this morning, with check-in staff managing to ward off any trouble.

While we are standing momentarily becalmed around check-in, Sarichka receives a call on her mobile telephone – although how anybody can remember the intergalactic number of her mobile is beyond me. Whenever I call her, I joke about how I'm trying to contact the troubled Mir Space Station with the help of an electrician's tip from my book entitled *Home Electrics for the Idiot*.

Struggling with the minute keys on her phone, Sarichka says, 'Jeremy, something's happening in Terminal 3, which they would like us to film. As reluctant as I am to leave you, I'll go over and be back as quickly as possible.' Watching Sarichka and the crew heading off on the almost ten-minute trek to Terminal 3 arrivals, I wonder what will happen to us while they are gone. Ironically, things have a habit of stirring into action while fly-on-the-wall film crews are nowhere to be seen!

As I glance at the relative tranquillity still surrounding check-in, my attention is drawn to a young lady sitting on top of her suitcase by the First Class desk. She appears to be breastfeeding her baby. Sure enough, as I walk towards her, my suspicions are confirmed. Not wanting to make her feel uncomfortable – she obviously doesn't anyway – I say, 'Sorry, madam, but do you mind if I get one of the staff to help you move to a less conspicuous place?' Fully expecting to be tongue-lashed for disturbing a moment of profound bonding with an offspring, I'm pleasantly surprised to hear the woman say, 'Sure. I was afraid to leave all my baggage unattended, and then the baby started making a hell of a din. I couldn't see any changing facilities nearby, so…' By the time she had finished confirming her willingness to move, a not insignificant queue had built up behind her. Russians, however, being what they are, appear to be at ease with such maternal situations, so much so that a couple helped the passenger to her feet while she continued to satisfy her baby's hungry cravings.

Having agreed to stand guard over the passenger's baggage while she goes with one of the staff to a more suitable place, I hear the Tsaritsa's voice saying over the radio, '241 in the zone for Fox 15.' Kasia is going to meet the aircraft, so I'm free to stay at check-in for a while.

Just as mother and baby return to get checked in, there is a phone call for me from Passenger Central Search. I don't believe it – two calls in two days! Surely not another knife-carrying passenger? This is getting boring. 'Hi there. Is it another passenger with a knife?' I ask, trying not to sound too nonplussed by events. 'No, it's better than that,' comes the reply from the security supervisor. 'Can you come upstairs to see us?' Now I'm intrigued and get the feeling that Sarichka is going to regret having taken the film crew off to Terminal 3. On my way upstairs, I let Kasia know where I'm going, 'Kashinka, just by way of a change, I'm off to Central Search to deal with another problem. Don't be surprised if I'm not downstairs at check-in when you go down there.'

Being no stranger to dealing with passengers at Central Search, as I'm sure you've already noticed, I am rarely shocked by what I see. But this one turns  out to be a first for me. Reaching the supervisor's desk next to the X-ray machines in departures, I am confronted by a middle-aged Russian lady sporting a highly bouffant carrot-coloured hairstyle and enough gold teeth to make Jaws look insignificant in the dentistry department. (Yes, humble apologies, Jaws is another of those famous James Bond characters. No need to ask what films I watched as a boy!)

The lady is clutching a large shopping bag, which appears to be moving about of its own free will. Trying hard not to look too unnerved by the sight of a wandering bag, I ask the security supervisor, 'What's up?' Attempting in turn to hide his surprise, he replies, 'This lady, who is due to travel on your 13.30 flight, has got a puppy in her hand baggage!' Regretfully, I discover it's not one of those clockwork toy puppies, it's the real living, breathing, chewing-slippers kind!

My translation skills are urgently required. 'Sorry, madam,' I commence, 'but might I ask why you have a puppy in your shopping bag?

And why you did not show it to the staff at check-in?' With a startling dazzle of highly polished teeth comes the reply in Russian, 'Well, I was given this dog by a friend the other day to take home. I always transport my animals around Moscow in such a bag. What's strange about that? I didn't think the check-in staff would worry about such a thing!' (I should explain that it's not uncommon in Russia to see pets being carried around in shopping bags. I, for one, have often seen this on the Moscow metro, but I've never before seen one being carried in a zipped-up bag through the departures area of Terminal 2!)

'Are you not aware of the need to produce various veterinary certificates, as well as provide the dog with a proper transportation box?' I enquire, knowing what response to expect. True to form, the by-now hysterical passenger says, 'My friend said not to worry about such things as they are not required ... why is everyone getting so excited about nothing?'

The events unfolding before me put me in mind of something that happened to Gabi about eighteen months ago. She had been standing at check-in minding her own business, as you do, when along came a passenger for Dhaka (a destination that we serve only once a week from Moscow, on Sundays) with an enormous St Bernard puppy on a lead. The passenger, a Rod Stewart lookalike, was amazed to learn that he needed to provide a special crate for the dog to travel in and that he was also required to furnish us with all the necessary paperwork from his vet and the dog's breeder. 'What d'you mean I can't take the dog with me on the lead?' he bellowed, failing to see the point.

After we had remained firm and refused to accept the dog, which, as I'm sure you can appreciate, was the only thing we could do, the passenger went off vowing to return in a week's time with everything in order. Sure enough, as promised, he arrived seven days later ... and then again seven days after that. Fourth time lucky! The message had finally sunk in and he turned up with everything we'd been asking for. The most puzzling thing, however, was that four days before he first attempted to travel, Aunty Pat had carefully briefed him over the phone as to what he would need to transport a St Bernard puppy. Funny old world, isn't it?

Returning to the dog-in-the-bag matter, I inform Jaws that I'm terribly sorry, but she will not be able to travel with the puppy like that. Jaws informs me that one of her Russian friends, who has just waved her off, may still be in the terminal. I'm sure you know by now that I love a challenge. Unfazed, I wander off to make an announcement in the very unlikely hope that the lady's friend is still somewhere in the terminal and will come forward to the information desk and retrieve the puppy. Blind faith is sometimes rewarded! The lady hears my announcement in the car park and comes rushing back, thinking that something has happened to her friend. Something has, but not what she thinks!

'Did you know your friend had a puppy in her bag?' I ask, suspecting that she may be the very person who has generously provided my passenger with this travelling companion. 'Yes, she purchased it yesterday from a breeder,' comes the reply in almost perfect English. Not quite the same story the passenger told us, but still… Relieved that here was a lady who seemed able to grasp the predicament, and was even willing to note down all our requirements and take the puppy home with her to make all the necessary travel arrangements for a later date, I wasn't about to quibble over a few variations in the puppy-in-a-bag plot. Lordy lord, at least the friend had sense! Jaws looked suitably satisfied with her friend's offer of assistance, but, uncontrite, she gave me and the security staff the evil eye.

Leaving Jaws, relieved of puppy-in-bag, to do battle with the other duty-free shoppers, I rush off to Gate 15. Thanks to the recurring nightmare of illegal  doggy transportation – and the need to ensure that all is well on the aircraft before we commence boarding – I'm already twenty minutes behind schedule. My spirits, however, are lifted by the crew on board our Airbus A310, who all appear to be in jolly mood. 'Everything's okay. The cleaners have finished, so we can start boarding if you're ready,' comes the cheerful news from the Chief Steward. Heading off towards the gate along the air-bridge, I respond with an equally cheery, 'Great, I'll start 'em off then.'

As the passengers file past me, I am stopped by the elderly knife-carrying gentleman from yesterday, who now looks more than pleased to be heading home. 'Young man,' he greets me, 'many thanks for all your help yesterday. I was very worried and confused by what was happening with the police. Of course, I had no idea that I wouldn't be allowed to take my knife with me.' To put him at his ease, I say, 'It was a pleasure, sir. I've spoken to your wife to assure her all is well and she and your son will be at the airport to meet you. Was everything okay at the police station? Did they find someone to translate for you?'

The Russian Embassy, it transpires, had stepped in to assist him, so all's well that ends well. Making his way towards the aircraft, the passenger thrusts his address into my hands and invites me to look him up for a glass of vodka next time I'm in Moscow.

Spying Marina at the end of the lounge, I immediately begin to offer a rendition of 'Aqua Marina' from *Stingray*. Not that our Marina is a subterranean mute, you understand. Far from it, she's a charming person. But for some reason, every time I see her I can't stop myself singing 'Marinnnnna, Aqua Marinnna, why…' etc., etc.

'How many down then, hon?' I ask, controlling myself. 'Seventeen at the moment, Jeremy, but Jo is out there rounding them up.' Working at Heathrow, you soon develop a sense of what it must have been like to be a cowboy in the days of the Great Wild West. As a boy aged about six, I used to love pretending I was Billy the Kid and the like, so maybe that's why I ended up in the Wild West of Hounslow! I often imagine a scene from *Bonanza* as the staff frantically chase around the lounge trying to herd up the stragglers.

I've got just four minutes before the 13.30 deadline and it's

✈ This is me during my 'I want to be a cowboy stage'. My mother obliged by making me this wonderful costume.

looking unlikely that we'll be ready in time. 'Marina, can we check with Jo if she's been to the pub yet?' No, Jo is not an alcoholic everybody! As incredible as it may seem, some passengers, oblivious that they are holding up an aircraft, develop the need to frequent the local watering hole just before departure. Jo confirms, *el supris*, that nine of the passengers are all sitting in the pub supping pints of ale. Fortunately, they have only managed to get two pints down, so are still capable of responding to staff directions and are running to the departure gate. These are the last of the missing seventeen to reach us, and as they come round the corner, the lounge begins to take on the appearance of a spit-and-sawdust saloon.

'Sorry, guys,' I shout as the men start heading for the phones scattered along the stretch of narrow lounge, 'there's no time to call your mothers. Can you go straight down, through the doors and then turn to the left, please?'

To check the head-count with the crew, I follow along behind the merry bunch. 'One hundred and seventy-eight, plus one baby?' I query, with a look of anticipation on my face. This is the moment when I begin to resemble an expectant father, wanting reassurance that all is well and that the crew agree with my passenger numbers. 'Just a moment. We're double-checking now,' comes the ever-so-cheerful reply from the Chief Steward.

Can you imagine? My mind is in overdrive: please come back and say 178, plus a baby, or even 179 total. I don't think I can stand a missing passenger at this stage in the proceedings. We are already fifteen minutes late and I'm very aware that Kasia's flight departed on time yesterday! 'We have 179, so all is okay.' Thanking God, I bid the crew a pleasant flight and watch as the door closes.

Having made my way back to the office without stopping for a chin-wag, I am surprised to see Sarichka and the film crew sitting with Kasia drinking coffee.
They'd been gone for so long, I'd assumed things had been so interesting across the other side of airport that they'd forgotten all about us in Terminal 2.

'Well? How did it go in Terminal 3 then?' I ask, hoping the trek was worth it. 'After the initial excitement, nothing much,' states Sarichka in her usual irrepressible bubbly manner. 'How about you, Jeremy?' 'You don't want to know,' I reply. 'I spent most of the time dealing with Moriarty and the hound of the Baskervilles.' As I relay the puppy-in-the-bag story, I note a certain regret on Sarichka's face. I knew something worthy of television would happen the minute they left and my intuition had been right.

As Sarichka and the crew decide to call it a day and head off to Costa Coffee to drown their sorrows in Colombian caffeine, I sit back at my desk and start to look through the various telexes and messages that have come in during my four-hour absence. The doctor from the embassy has called, but when I ring back, I'm out of luck because he has already left for the day. The stretcher-case details will have to wait until tomorrow. There is, however, good news – a message from St Petersburg confirming the availability of a stretcher. One less hurdle to overcome before D-Day!

Empress Kashinka leaves the office just after 4 p.m. and I'm able to plough through some more correspondence while I wait for the 18.10 arrival of SU582 from Tokyo and Moscow. All the telexes concerning the flight have come through and the aircraft is expected to land about ten minutes ahead of schedule. So, all being well, I'll be able to leave the office by 19.00 hours.

Reservations close down at 17.30 and, as usual, our phones suddenly become busy again as people call in to reconfirm details, request vegetarian meals, or check up on the arrival time of the aircraft. So busy are the phones that I have to abandon my paperwork and go to help Igor deal with the callers.

Flight SU582 enters the all-important zone at 17.50 and is allocated the dreaded far-flung Echo 40 parking stand. I decide to call airfield operations – the people who allocate the parking stands – in the hope that I might be able to persuade them to change Echo 40 for something a little bit nearer. 'Hi. It's Aeroflot here. Our 582 has just entered the zone. Is there any chance of improving on Echo 40?' Knowing that our aircraft has the dubious honour of being the first of the night-stoppers to arrive and one of the last to depart in the morning, I'm not optimistic that airfield ops will oblige. 'Sorry,' the controller predictably informs me, 'there's no chance, I'm afraid.'

It really is a dog's life … This means that while I will be able to hitch a lift with Igor to the Echo 40 stand, I will still need to walk the equivalent of half a London marathon with the passengers through Passport Control to make sure that all's well, and that none of them gets held by Her Majesty's Immigration service.

Having waited until all the 18.05 arrivals collect their baggage and make their way from the airport, I head back to my car. I'm completely whacked, but still relatively unscathed by the events of the past three days. Day Four is normally when I begin to feel the pinch, so arriving home at just after 9 p.m., I head straight for bed, praying I will not pre-empt the delights to come by dreaming about the next few days ahead.

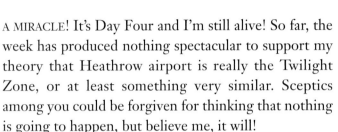

CHAPTER 4

IT NEVER RAINS BUT IT POURS

A MIRACLE! It's Day Four and I'm still alive! So far, the week has produced nothing spectacular to support my theory that Heathrow airport is really the Twilight Zone, or at least something very similar. Sceptics among you could be forgiven for thinking that nothing is going to happen, but believe me, it will!

I never had any desire to follow in my father's footsteps and become a member of Her Majesty's Royal Navy, so finding myself almost sailing to work this morning as I aquaplane through a torrential downpour is a very unpleasant feeling. This is no time to be driving along in the all-too-familiar automatic mode, thinking about the day ahead. I need all my concentration to avoid the Neanderthal drivers who have managed to get out of bed at the same time as me. The weather has sprouted more people than usual who drive along in the outside lane at 100 mph flashing their lights, as well as those terribly careful, considerate drivers (yes, sarcasm is intended) who love sitting in the middle lane chugging along at 45 mph and thinking they are bullet-proof. There's plenty of 'em out there. I've just managed to avoid at least twenty-five of them!

✈ 'A little to the left, down a bit, no, up a bit, steady, that's it. FIRE!' No, I'm not on the *Golden Shot* (a very old game show). My colleague Giles and I are positioning the airbridge on to the awaiting aircraft.

Another early-morning arrival at work can mean only one thing – a flight scheduled to leave for Moscow at 09.00. As I drive through the cargo tunnel that links the south side of the airport with the central area, the business of the day comes rushing back to me: two flights to Moscow, a stretcher case to finalize for Saturday, a visit to our caterers to complete an equipment inventory and, in between, a mountainous pile of paperwork to carry on plodding through.

Oh, no – not again! I really must find myself a decent cartographer. Perhaps someone from the Ordnance Survey could help? My usual path to the office block, which is adjacent to the terminal building, has been boarded in and there is one of those awfully polite notices apologizing for the obvious inconvenience caused. Why is it that those signs somehow never seem to make you feel any better? I'm now faced with the prospect of having to go outside and get drenched in the downpour as I make my way via the main entrance of the terminal and dash along the front of the building to the office. Not a great distance, I admit, but far enough to get wet.

Heading to the office looking like I've just swum the English Channel fully clothed, my feet slurp inside my shoes. Please let the air conditioning be functioning properly – I don't want to walk in and find Aunty Pat frozen blue with teeth chattering. But no, a blissfully cool oasis hits me as I open the door and it's all thanks to those unsung heroes in the engineering department, who've battled through the night to ensure that everything is back in order. Pat, having completed the preliminary jobs of the shift (such as printing off the day's battle plan), is filling up the coffee-maker and looking considerably more relaxed than she did when she finished duty on Monday.

'Have you had a good few days off, Patsy?' I ask, seeing from the remnants of paint left in her hair that she has been busy. 'I've managed to finish decorating the hallway and I'm really pleased with the result,' Patsy replies, adding, 'Jeremy, I need to ask you for a favour? Could you possibly stay at my place tomorrow night and look after the cats? Adrian and I are going to a dinner party and would like not to have to worry about coming home. If it's okay with you, I'll come straight to work in the morning from my friends' home.'

✈ Pat reads over my list of 'demands' in exchange for my services as a cat-sitter. Judging by the look on her face, I may have to rethink my needs. The champagne and caviar aren't absolutely essential, I suppose...

Pat is a bit like yours truly and loves cats. But, unlike me, she's a member of her local Cats Protection League and fosters homeless cats and kittens. At any one time, you might expect to find at least fifteen moggies running amok in her house, which for some people would be too much, especially after a hard day's work. But, as every Friday night I normally spend the better part of four hours sitting on the M25, one of the country's largest concrete car parks, the thought of reaching West Drayton in a little over ten minutes from Heathrow is heaven-sent. 'Pat,' I reply, 'don't worry. I'd love to look after the little beasties for you.' (Incidentally, I bet National Car Parks wishes it owned that glorious feat of British engineering called the M25. Just imagine what it could charge drivers for the pleasure of sitting there!)

Pat's problem sorted, I pick up the daily report to see what's in store. Why did I bother? The afternoon flight, SU242, is overbooked by fifteen passengers! Okay, I know some of you will be thinking, why do airlines overbook flights? Well, that's simple: it's because there are always a number of people who, having booked, fail to turn up to travel. The sad thing is that if passengers phoned to cancel unwanted reservations, then the practice of overbooking aircraft would be considerably reduced, if not eradicated.

Under normal circumstances, fifteen passengers would not really cause a problem, but most of today's flyers have purchased a fixed date group fare, which means that they must fly today or forfeit the ticket. It is possible, therefore, that everyone who's booked *will* arrive at the airport! Already, I can see that things are beginning to look darker than yesterday.

 Some inconsiderate person has switched up the volume on the main unit of our radio system and Gabi's voice suddenly booms over the airwaves and wakes us all up. 'Pat from Gabi. When you come down to check-in, could you please bring some more First Class lounge invites with you?' Frantically trying to stretch over the desk to turn the volume down, I volunteer to go to check-in, thus leaving Aunty Pat to make her way to the far-flung corners of the airport and take charge of passengers arriving at the dreaded Echo 40 stand!

Now, I don't want you to think that I'm being lazy and trying to get out of traipsing to the other side of the airport. Truth is, I have to meet Igor outside the terminal at 08.45 in order to head off to catering. So volunteering to go to check-in is very sensible, or at least I think it is. Grabbing about fifty lounge invites from the cupboard, I head off into the terminal.

Because of the building work, which reminds me a lot of Russia – where most buildings at the moment seem to be under *remont* (the Russian word for repair) – I'm forced to navigate my way through the

Heathrow equivalent of Channel 4's *Crystal Maze*. At least by accepting the challenge of the maze, I avoid drowning-by-rain on the street.

The terminal is already heaving with people and it's not even 8 a.m. Security is busy trying to process what appears to be the entire people-content of Wembley Stadium through its already over-burdened metal detectors. I am not the only one, it seems, beginning to feel the pressure build up as we head towards the weekend.

Greeting the check-in staff with my usual cheery 'Morning folks. Are we all all right?', I can see that the staff are feeling the strain of a long tour of duty, as none of them is able to offer a beaming smile – just a crack of the lips through which quiet greetings emerge. Things are about to change, though. Mr Clark, a passenger in his early fifties, approaches one of the girls on check-in wanting to know where he can pick up a TOD. (Oops, code. You must admit I've been doing pretty well at keeping them to a minimum. Anyway, TOD is a Ticket On Departure). 'Just over there, sir. Aeroflot's ticket desk is next to Lufthansa,' answers the staff member. 'Excellent. I'll just go and get my baggage from my son's car,' exclaims Mr Clark.

Always wanting to help, I say, 'Don't worry about your ticket, Mr Clark, I'll go over and collect it for you. Just bring yourself straight back to check-in with your baggage.' Mr Clark duly disappears into the pond-like conditions surrounding the terminal and almost twenty minutes later returns with four enormous check-patterned bags.

Sorry to distract you, but I cannot let this moment pass, without saying something about the kind of luggage Mr Clark is carrying. Have you ever seen those enormous plastic bags that are sold in markets for a couple of quid? They normally have a blue and red pseudo tartan appearance and are capable of carrying a person's entire worldly possessions. Well, they're the bane of the airline world! East Europeans, among many others, love them. They don't weigh anything, but by the Lord Harry, can you pack stuff in 'em!

Our drenched passenger, Mr Clark, is distressed to learn that he has packed nigh on 60 kilos into his four bags. He is allowed 20 free kilos and is travelling to Tokyo, so the remainder will cost him around £800. 'I'll leave one of them with my son, who's still outside washing the car,' he informs me.

Hang on a minute, did I hear him properly? Could his son *really* be outside Terminal 2 washing his car in the pouring rain? This I cannot believe. But just when you think you've seen it all, something comes along to dispel that idea. Trying not to sound as though I doubt his word, I offer some crafty assistance. This, I must see. Sure enough, Mr Clark's son is outside with a sponge in his hand, illegally parked and washing his car. God knows how he's avoided being moved on and heaven knows where he found the bucket of hot soapy water! People do the strangest things at the airport.

 Igor arrives just in the nick of time to rescue me from trying to solve the mystery. Now, I'm able to leave my beleaguered colleagues to gather everyone up, including Mr Clark, who managed to pay for some of his excess while his son continued to polish the car. As we drive to Feltham, the location of our catering supplier, LSG Skychef (a business unit of Lufthansa German Airlines), I tell Igor all about the wonders of working with the Great Travelling Public – something that he rarely has to do. Perhaps I should have tried to enjoy school more; perhaps, then, I could have been the engineer and he could have been the troubled traffic supervisor.

Compiling an inventory of catering equipment is, take my word for it, as boring as it sounds. But unfortunately, it's a necessary evil that needs to be done at least once a month. Unless we count how many cups, plates, trays, cutlery packs, glasses, etc. are on station, we will end up running out. I, for one, don't even want to think what life would be like trying to beg, steal or borrow 300-plus tray set-ups (the term used to describe all the equipment on one passenger meal tray).

The trip to catering also gives me the opportunity to try to find out why my crusty bread rolls (from two days ago) went AWOL. Not surprisingly, the supervisor is sticking to the story that the rolls were loaded and must, therefore, have been on board the aircraft somewhere. I decide not to explain that our very own Colonel Kleb, on account of her incredible efficiency, does not miss things like several hundred bread rolls.

Happy in the knowledge that we have enough equipment to survive until the next delivery from Moscow, we head back to the car. The sun has finally decided to grace us with its presence. Although my spirits are lifted by the sudden brightness, I'm not lulled into thinking that things are going to be easy back at the terminal.

Before heading off to deal with the marauding masses on the ground floor, there's time to grab a quick cuppa and speak with the Russian Embassy  doctor about Saturday's stretcher passenger. Once again, my luck's not in. The doctor's busy with his morning consultations. 'Gorskii,' I say to Igor, 'could you do me a favour mate? I need to speak with the embassy doctor about Saturday's little bit of fun, but he's not available at the moment. Could you possibly ring him in about half an hour? The file is on my desk. I just need the final medical report to send to St Petersburg.' Igor agrees to call, leaving me free to go down to check-in.

The terminal is now bursting at the seams with people. As I make my way across the concourse through the crowds, I'm reminded of the multitude of nationalities that pass through Terminal 2. It may seem crazy, but after working at Heathrow for a while, you begin to develop a sixth sense about where a person comes from. How on earth, I hear you ask, can you tell a passenger's nationality without seeing his or her passport, or hearing him or her speak? First, the baggage and the clothes tend to be giveaways, then there's the shoes. Daft, I know, but by and large I can tell an East European from his or her footwear alone.

Virtually every nationality has developed stereotypical behaviour patterns. Nigerians, for example, arrive – usually dressed smartly in suits, etc. – with the biggest suitcases you've ever seen and matching hand-baggage piled high on trolleys, and then insist they've no money to pay for excess baggage. People from north Africa tend to be similar, although their clothing and powers of persuasion are slightly

✈ OVERLEAF Driving airside certainly has its advantages, especially if the aircraft is parked up in the Twilight Zone, or if time is rapidly running out for me. Safety is the key when driving on the tarmac, even if time is of the essence.

less formal and business-like. The Brits habitually let problems stock-pile as they wait patiently in queues, and then suddenly explode at the most inopportune moment. This is a topic that I could go on about all day. It's fascinating to watch how various nationalities conduct themselves, and I, of course, have a bird's-eye view, but unfortunately it's time to get to check-in.

The ground floor is awash with people and their luggage. Every queue is stretching to the back of the hall and tempers are beginning to fray. Aeroflot's queue is no exception. True to form, most of the Russians are attempting to stand in a semi-circle around the check-in desks. Very few of our Russian passengers speak English, so they usually rely either on a tour leader or yours truly to translate for them. They have developed this knack of standing in a huddle, trying to hear anything and everything being said in their mother tongue. Who can blame them, really? But it's an awesome sight – a humble check-in agent ringed by 300 passengers, all eager to obtain their boarding cards and make their way to the duty free shops, or the VAT reclaim area.

Making – correction – *fighting* my way through the hordes of people, I suddenly feel as though I'm in the Far East. The queue has taken on the look of a Vietnamese street market, where traders sell everything from old tank parts to freshly prepared oriental cuisine (something, by the way, that I *really* love – no, not the old tank parts, the food!). We have three flights a week to Hanoi from Moscow and yes, you've guessed it, today is one of them.

A group of twenty-six Vietnamese passengers is desperately trying to rearrange its baggage in a bid to cut down the weight. They have come up against Marie-Claude, who is being her usual super-efficient self. However, as my French colleague throws down the baggage gauntlet to our passengers, I'm anxious to avoid the queue stagnating. Acutely aware of the need to support staff members, I also know that, with time running out, a compromise is necessary.

'*Bon* morning, gorgeous! How much baggage do they have in total love?' I ask, not wanting to make my colleague feel undermined by my presence. Marie-Claude has been struggling with them for forty minutes and the last thing she wants is for me to be soft with them. In addition, the flight is full and loading space is at a premium. 'I've already allowed them up to 25 kilos each, plus one piece of hand-baggage at 7 kilos,' comes Marie-Claude's helpful reply, 'but they still have 40 kilos of excess.'

Turning to the group leader, I say, 'My colleague is correct to charge you, sir. She has already been more than generous. However, as I need to get the queue moving again, I'm prepared to offer an exceptional compromise and allow you an additional 20 kilos for the whole group. Even so, you'll need to leave one of the bags behind – unless, of course, you are able to pay for the remaining 20 kilos.' My compromise seems to have worked. They are happy to leave one bag with a friend and Marie-Claude is not looking daggers at me (not that she would, anyway, you understand).

Our Ilyushin IL86 aircraft, seating 316 passengers, is parked on stand Golf 12, having arrived just five minutes behind schedule at 12.05. In less than an hour this mighty beast should be lifting off again for Moscow with a full load of passengers, plus three tons of cargo, a ton of mail and 500 kilos of specialist courier baggage from Virgin. The crew of fifteen are enjoying a short respite before the 13.00 boarding deadline.

Pat has been run ragged on the ticket desk processing last-minute ticket amendments, dealing with excess baggage enquiries and giving out arrival information to callers. Gabi has been office-bound since 10.00 this morning, catching up on her paperwork and answering the phones with the assistance of Harry, who, in turn, is juggling the rosters around trying to fit in everyone's holiday requests. My old mate, Igor, a specialist on the Ilyushin IL86, is in his element running around the aircraft completing his line-maintenance checks and ensuring the aircraft is fully airworthy for the return leg to Moscow.

Where am I in all of this? Need you ask? I'm still at check-in! A record twenty-four minutes before closure (this being the phrase used

✈ OVERLEAF Just before departure I check with our engineering expert, Igor, that all's well and that we're ready for pushback. More importantly, I check to make sure he hasn't tried to stow away in a secret compartment. The other two chaps are my henchmen, preventing Igor's escape.

to describe the time at which check-in finishes and control of the flight passes to the staff at the departure gate) the aircraft is full. Twenty First Class, fifty-six Business Class and 240 Economy Class passengers, plus a baby, have managed to make their way through the bedlam that is check-in, are already sitting in the departure lounge, or merrily picking up those last-minute bargains from duty free. So why have I still got a group of Russians at check-in? Yes, the overbooking problem I spotted first thing this morning! Someone in Moscow, whose job it is to study travelling trends and decide by how many passengers a particular flight should be overbooked, has sadly got his or her sums wrong today. Three hundred and twenty-three passengers, bless them, have arrived for the flight.

At last a problem I can get my teeth into! It's at times like this that the weak among us quiver in a corner and pray that the ground will open up and swallow them, but not me! I *love* a challenge, as I am sure you've discovered as you've journeyed with me through the week. Seven overbooked passengers are nothing. I've now got to work with Pat to find a quick solution to this problem, but first I need to explain to the seven waiting passengers what's happening.

'I'm terribly sorry, but the flight is already full.' Before I have a chance to say what I want to do to help them, one passenger says in Russian, 'How is that possible? We have a confirmed booking on the flight? This makes no sense.' At this point you should remember that until 1991 very few Russians travelled abroad, so these types of budget-flight problems are all new to them. Domestic travel in the former Soviet Union is so very different.

Replying in Russian, in complete sympathy with their plight, I state, 'Unfortunately, our colleagues in Moscow who control the availability of flights have miscalculated and we are now going to have to re-route you via another city in Europe.' The passengers are now completely confused. Why, if they had a flight booked direct from London, do they now have to go via another city to Moscow? 'If you give me five minutes, I'll go and sort out your new travel arrangements. I'll need all of your tickets, please.' The passengers reluctantly hand me their tickets as I ask one of the AFSL staff to wait with them, just in case they need to be rushed to another terminal.

Over at the ticket desk, I'm able to check the availability of flights to Moscow via other destinations. 'Patsy, we've ended up with seven over. Can we have a look in the system at the best connection, please?' Patsy responds immediately by tapping ferociously on the keyboard. 'The only real connection is via Paris with British Midland and then on to an SU flight [SU being the two-letter flight designator of Aeroflot – Russian International Airlines],' comes the reply from my less-than-relaxed-looking colleague. 'What time does the flight leave here, hon?' I ask, praying that we've got time to rush them to Terminal 1, from where British Midland operates to Paris.

Pat, by this time, is busy filling in an FIM (Flight Interruption Manifest), which, in basic terms, is a document issued to passengers in place of a ticket so that they can travel on another airline. It is specifically used in circumstances such as that confronting us at the moment. 'It leaves in just under twenty-five minutes, Jeremy.'

As Aunty Pat hands me the FIM, I ask Ash, a fit colleague from our handling agent, AFSL, to run with my unfortunate passengers to Terminal 1, which, if they sprint, will take about fifteen minutes. Fortunately, the group members are all fairly young and don't have too much baggage, so they should make it. 'Ash,' I say, 'I'll give Midland a call and tell them that you're on your way with the passengers.' Almost before I've had a chance to finish speaking, Ash has ushered the passengers into a huddle to run together. One or two of them continue to protest that they don't understand what is going on, while the remainder thank me and dash off like something from *Challenge Anneka* towards Terminal 1.

Leaving Pat to tidy up the ticket desk, I rush off to the departure gate. I'm already nearly half an hour late getting there, so I run through the departure  lounge, which certainly gives the onlookers a good laugh. It's not often you see a real-life Michelin Man doing such an impressive sprint through an airport!

As I try to catch my breath, I'm informed that all is going well and that boarding should be on time at one o'clock. Taking my radio, I contact Igor, our very own Stalin lookalike, hoping that he won't detect my breathless state, 'Gor … from Jemskii.' My hopes are dashed when he replies, 'Oh, what a to-do! Have you been running, Mr General Secretary, you snake?' 'Yes, all right, thank you very much, Gorinskii. Are you all set down there? I'd like to start boarding as soon as I can breathe normally again.' I should have known better than to say something like that to Igor, who always manages to find just the right sarcastic retort: 'If we're waiting for you to be normal, we'll never be able to board!' As I look through the window at my foolish friend laughing back at me from the ramp, he makes a thumbs-up signal, which can only mean that they have finished loading the fuel and that the cleaners are clear of the aircraft. We're set to board!

After making the flight boarding announcements, I have time to catch up with the current state of play. In just under twenty minutes we should have the door of the aircraft closed, so I'm pleased to learn from the staff that we are just eleven passengers down, of which eight are First Class and will probably be sat in the First Class lounge, which is very conveniently situated next to Gate 12. 'Can we check with the CIP [the AFSL lounge] and ask them to send whoever's in there for the flight to the gate, please?' One of the staff immediately picks up the phone, but before we know it, a group of eight are being led round the corner by Boris, our Station Manager. It turns out that they are a group of military officials who have been on an exchange organized by the British Government. Hot in pursuit are two other missing passengers who have been waiting at VAT reclaim for a refund. So, ten found – one still missing.

Time is running out. There are now only six minutes to go before push-back, so I need to speed up the pace at the boarding gate. 'Okay, can I just confirm we're still one down at the moment, please?' I ask. 'Yeah – just the one down at the moment,' comes the standard response from the staff. 'Do we have the correct number of flight

---

✈ From these windows I can see all that is going on, which is vital if I am to adhere to my tight schedule. The loading of the aircraft needs to be precise. I glance at my watch and pray that everything is how it should be. Then and only then will there be time to read the latest copy of *Planespotters' Monthly*.

coupons?' Answering in the affirmative, Martine, the team leader, adds, 'We're just checking on board now for the last missing passenger and someone's pacing the lounge with the Aeroflot sign trying to spot the person.' Martine is thinking at the same speed as I am, which is no surprise as she is one of AFSL's more experienced members of staff, and works very well at the departure gate pulling her team together.

We've now established that the missing passenger is a female who arrived at Heathrow earlier this morning on a flight from Toronto. She went through the FCC (Flight Connections Centre) and should, in theory, have been sitting in the departure lounge for nigh on four hours clutching her boarding card (upon which the departure time of the flight is clearly written). 'Can we check with the staff member who dealt with her at the FCC? They may be able to remember what she looked like,' I say, trying not to sound desperate. There are now just two minutes before departure, and she is nowhere to be seen. Martine informs me that, unfortunately, the staff member concerned has already finished his shift.

The dispatcher, who is responsible for co-ordinating all the AFSL staff dealing with the flight, joins us. 'Okay, Nick,' I greet him, 'there's no sign of our missing punter, so we need to start the baggage caper, please.' Nick doesn't want to hear this. It means that he and the ramp staff are going to have to locate the missing passenger's baggage on board the aircraft and then remove it for security reasons. Martine informs Nick that the missing passenger checked in two pieces in Toronto and gives him the tag numbers.

After just eight minutes of searching, the team leader on the ramp manages to locate the container with the two bags (the containers are those metal igloo-like objects into which we place most of the baggage, thus making the loading and unloading of wide-bodied aircraft easier). This means that we can now remove the passenger's name from the flight list and leave for Moscow without her. I know this sounds harsh, but we have no way of knowing how long it will be before she turns up or we locate her, and I, for one, am not prepared to delay the flight indefinitely.

'Gorskii,' I say to Igor, 'they've located the lost passenger's baggage and it's been off-loaded.' Acknowledging my message, Igor closes the door to one of the aircraft's holds. The crew are given all the paperwork by Nick and, just fourteen minutes behind schedule, the aircraft is cleared to push back.

While Martine prints off a copy of the passenger manifest for me, I stand watching the aircraft through the window. Just as the flight deck crew are  running through their final checks, prior to moving into the queue for take-off, the door to the departure gate swings open and in comes a woman with dripping wet hair. 'Hello. Is this the gate for flight SU242?' asks the lady with the wet locks in relatively clear English. Can you imagine – fifteen minutes after boarding has ended, our missing passenger – a Mrs Zaitsaeva – has decided to put in an appearance.

'Madam, you're too late,' declares Martine, resisting the temptation to ask the passenger why she has dripping wet hair. 'The aircraft has just left.' I am not so reticent, 'Excuse me, madam, but might I ask where you have been since you arrived this morning? I've had a whole team of people scouring the terminal in search of you, not to mention six calls put out over the PA system. Did you not hear your name being called? Our aircraft was forced to depart late because you failed to arrive on time.'

Half expecting the passenger to go on the attack, accusing us – or some other airport official – for leaving her stranded, I'm almost speechless to hear her say, 'I've been in Terminal 1 having a shower, or at least that's where I think the shower was. I'm terribly sorry. I lost track of time. Can you get the aircraft back?'

It's my turn to restrain myself and to resist the temptation to say something unforgivable to Mrs Zaitsaeva. It's almost unimaginable – wouldn't you say? – a passenger calmly having a shower while her flight is departing! At this point, I'd like to reiterate that people really do do the strangest things at Heathrow and that this is what has led me to believe that we live in some kind of mysterious Bermuda-like triangle. Think I'm exaggerating? Well, there's still time for me to show you the error of your ways. We've still got three days of the shift left to survive!

Martine offers to escort Mrs Zaitsaeva to the baggage reclaim area so that, having picked up her bags, she can make her way to one of Heathrow's many hotels. I am left praying that, by tomorrow, Mrs Zaitsaeva will have learned an invaluable lesson and will arrive in plenty of time for the 11 a.m. flight, having showered *before* she leaves for the airport!

 Back in the office, a full medical report from the embassy doctor is awaiting me on my desk. At long last, just for a change, something seems to be coming together. Sure enough, the passenger will be secured to a stretcher, with his head strapped between a neck support to protect his spine. The remainder of the report gives a breakdown of the drugs etc. administered to the patient. I fax the report to St Petersburg and await their response.

As – in a bid to boost my energy levels – I pour myself a cup of coffee, Ash walks into the office. Still looking as fit as a fiddle, she tells me that all went well with our overbooked passengers. Thankfully, they survived the sprint and are all winging their way to Paris. Having thanked my athletic colleague, I move over to the computer and send a telex to our staff at Charles de Gaulle Airport, Paris, to ensure that they will be on hand to assist the passengers when the British Midland flight lands.

Gabi has finished for the day, and Pat is assembling all the documents from the afternoon flight that will need to be sent to Moscow for processing. Igor is keen to head off to the Excelsior Hotel to partake of the gym facilities, so bids us a pleasant evening. Harry, who has managed to finalize the holiday roster, has gone off for a meeting with our aircraft cleaning company and is not expected back until tomorrow.

'Enough's enough, Patsy. Let's go home. Tomorrow we've got more of the same, I'm sure.' Pat doesn't need much encouragement – she's as bushed as I am, and needs to get home to feed all the cats. So at just after 4 p.m. we leave for the day.

Driving home, I suddenly remember that I'm due to have dinner with Natasha at the university. She's promised to cook me some of my favourite Russian dishes, and a few of her students will be joining us. Natasha and I normally manage to put the world to rights when we get together, so the thought of spending a Russian-style evening with my friend carries me home on a wave of anticipation.

Clutching jars of Marmite (a strange gift, I grant you, but Natasha's family love it and I know she'll appreciate that more than flowers – especially as she had flowers on Tuesday when she arrived), I arrive at the university, which is just a fifteen-minute drive from my home. I'm greeted by a very glamorous-looking Natasha, who has gathered all her novice students for an enlightening What-Makes-Russia-Tick? evening. '*Zaichik, prakhadi,*' my dear friend greets me, ordering me into the flat for supper. The evening is packed full of debate as the students try to understand the ins and outs of Russia. I don't profess to be an expert by any means, but I hope I understand better than most why Russia is such an amazing country.

During the evening I discover another reason why Natasha's baggage was so heavy when she arrived. She has managed to bring two bottles of my favourite Georgian wine with her. Many of the students are experiencing Russian hospitality, which I think is second to none, for the first time and seem delighted by my friend's efforts to make them feel at home. 'Natash, it's time for me to go. It's after eleven already. And although I could sit here all night chatting, I do need to get up and go to work in the morning. However, as promised, I'll be back on Monday to take you for your favourite fish and chips dinner by the sea.'

I reach home to find the cats – Lenin and Rasputin – sitting by the garage eagerly awaiting my return. They also want to go to bed. Tomorrow's another day …

AFSL

CHAPTER 5

THAT SINKING FEELING

AFTER JUST FOUR AND A HALF HOURS' SLEEP, the alarm signals the start of yet another day – Granny's overslept! I've never been the type to roll over and grab an extra twenty minutes sleep, but this morning I really have to fight the temptation. I've yet to pack my overnight bag for Pat's.

Friday, when the M25 is even more murderous than usual, tends to be the one day of the week when I travel to work by train. The journey takes three hours to complete, but is decidedly less stressful than driving. However, the weekend service from Liverpool Street station is so awful that today I'm forced to do the norm and sit behind the wheel in order to avoid the hassle of travelling home by train from Pat's tomorrow. Surprisingly, the roads appear to be fairly clear, and for the first time this week I reach work in good time, completely relaxed.

✈ 'Igor, who the hell is that enormous great bloke down there? We have remembered to pay our aircraft parking fees, haven't we? Did you manage to upset anyone this morning when you came into work?' All's well. It appears that two military officials from Russia have just pulled up in an embassy limousine and are flying off to Moscow aboard our Tupolev TU 154M. They've been lucky enough to pass through the Hounslow Suite, avoiding the hordes at check-in, although I'm not sure that all their baggage is acceptable, even if they are built like T34 tanks.

FRIDAY

07:00 Just as I go to sit down, having checked that neither of the two Moscow flights of the day are overbooked, I discover a poster lying on my desk. As I unroll it, I'm delighted to see the faces of the Politburo members from the 1980 Central Committee of the Soviet Union – Gorbachev, Andropov, Gromyko and Shevardnadze, to mention just four of the many famous people. But … hang on a minute, something's not quite right with the poster. Where's Leonid Brezhnev, the General Secretary of the Party? A closer examination reveals that Igor has doctored the poster. There, sat in Brezhnev's position, is a photograph of yours truly! The sight of me sitting at the head of the Politburo is just the tonic I need to get me started.

✈ Igor's handiwork, recognizing my status as General Secretary. He has imposed my photo on a poster of the 1980 Politburo Central Committee of the Soviet Union.

Before preparing today's report, I need to read through the telexes that have come in overnight. Among the passenger lists, catering figures and flight movement signals is a message from our cargo department in Moscow. Staff there have loaded twenty pieces of high-value cargo on to our SU243 flight, which should be landing at Heathrow in less than two and a half hours.

The cargo turns out to be a load of old carbon – almost fifteen million pounds worth of diamonds for De Beers to be precise, which is even more than Caprice has belly buttons for! Thoughts of the Brinks Mat robbery spring to mind as I organize our security company to meet the flight and transfer the diamonds safely to Customs. A cunning plan will be needed if I'm going to purloin a few of the glittering gems for myself and avoid having to work this weekend! Would anyone notice if I suddenly developed a limp through walking with the weight of a girl's best friend in my pocket?

Dispensing with the idea almost immediately on account of not knowing what I would do with a girl's best friend even if I had one, my thoughts turn to my ancestors. No, truly, there is a connection. Prior to the Bolshevik Revolution in Russia, my family were big in diamonds and silver and ran some of the country's mines. Now that's a thought! Maybe now's the time I should lay claim to my inheritance and convince De Beers that the Russian Government has decided to restore property and goods seized by Lenin's revolutionaries, and the shipment is, in fact, for me.

Thoughts of not-so-petty theft are soon wiped away as the door swings open and in comes Pat with the Lipstick Goddess hot on her heels. Kasia, as always, hangs her coat up in the cupboard and then checks in the mirror that all is well in her make-up department. That done, she sits down and prepares the daily report for us. Pat is beaming from ear to ear, safe in the knowledge that she has temporarily transferred the responsibility for her feline charges to me, the General Secretary. The girls haven't seen each other for a few days and spend twenty minutes or so catching up on the latest gossip, while I continue to read through the telexes.

Information has arrived from St Petersburg concerning our stretcher case tomorrow. They are confident that all's well, although I

still have this nagging feeling that there is something that somebody is not telling me. It often strikes me when reading newspapers that East Europeans seem to have a very different attitude towards life than most other people. I remember seeing an article in a Russian newspaper just after the collapse of the Soviet Union concerning a group of thirty or so Belorussians who had crossed the Polish border in a clapped-out bus to do some shopping. Not long after entering Poland, three of the group died from the excitement of looking for bargains. The remainder, it was alleged, then elected to leave the three corpses on the bus while they completed their four-day tour. After all, they'd reasoned, if they did this, they'd be able to take the duty-free allowance of their dead comrades with them when crossing the border back into Belorussia!

Kasia's drawn the short straw this morning and finds herself elected to staff the ticket desk. Some days, when nobody wants a ticket, being on the ticket

counter is like sitting in a graveyard. The inactivity is almost too much to bear. The Tsaritsa and I often joke that we are going to turn the desk into one of those famous Russian street kiosks, which have a tiny little window through which to pass all purchases and where it's possible to buy everything from bread and milk to a twelve-volt battery for your car.

Picking up her manicure set – well, give the girl a break, she does need to while away a bit of time – Kasia leaves the office. Head hung low, looking like something at the front of a Russian funeral cortège, she plods her way downstairs. Not wanting to gloat too much, I utter, 'Enjoy, Kashinka, we all know how much you love being on the "Show Case" [the name given by our colleague, Harry, to our newly opened ticket desk].'

There's just over an hour before our diamond-encrusted Airbus is due to touch down. It being Harry's day off, Pat has volunteered to

Help! Pascale (from AFSL) and I trying to locate a missing piece of baggage in the depths of Terminal 2.

stay by the phones, so I'm free to pop over to Terminal 3 for a quick cuppa with another of the BBC's *Airport* subjects – Michelle Harris.

Driving airside between terminals, which, incidentally, is a bit like navigating your way around Britain's 'B' roads, I receive a gentle reminder of the on-going building works. My usual route from the office has a diversion in place, which involves enough roundabouts to make Milton Keynes look naked, and I find myself driving almost as far as Staines reservoir to reach the Terminal 3 Control Room, where Michelle is already well into her early shift.

Banging on the door, on account of it having a splendiferous security code, I can see Michelle staring at a bank of television monitors. A vibration passes through the door handle as my comrade lets me into the secret world of 'Big Brother'. Baikanour Cosmodrome and Cape Canaveral eat your hearts out: Terminal 3 Control Room, from where Michelle, the Duty Officer, is charged with monitoring security, safety and passenger through-put, has enough equipment to sustain an entire space programme.

'How's it going, love?' I enquire of my friend, who is busy watching passengers getting in and out of one of the terminal's many lifts on the CCTV. (More code, although I'm sure Closed Circuit TV is a familiar one for you all, given that virtually every major town and city in Britain has now invested in this surveillance gear.) 'Fine. How's you? Sarah was here yesterday with the film crew. Have you seen much of her yet?' comes the effervescent reply.

I ought to point out that there is no on-camera jealousy or rivalry between myself and Michelle. We are simply eager to know how each other's television careers are coming along. 'Yeah,' I respond, 'they were with me on Wednesday, but had to come over here to film some marvellous event. Do you know what it was all about? Sarichka didn't say a great deal, other than it was all a waste of time.'

Wednesday, Michelle informs me, was her rest day, so she hasn't a clue what all the excitement was about. Just as we start to discuss Michelle's fortieth birthday celebrations, she receives a call advising her of a Code 93 in the departures area of the building. Code 93 means only one thing – an unattended bag! Why people insist on walking off without taking their baggage with them is beyond me. Michelle duly dispatches one of her colleagues, who is already roaming around the building trouble-shooting, to investigate this latest call. '243 in the zone for Golf 14,' interrupts Aunty Pat's voice over the radio. 'Sorry, Michelle,' I say, 'I have to go. Maybe we can get together for a proper chat early next week?'

Feeling like Zebedee on his magic roundabout, I speed off at 20 mph (this being the maximum speed limit airside at Heathrow), leaving Michelle with the all-clear call from her colleague. Ironically, as I pull up next to Golf 14, our Airbus in Diamond Sakha livery pulls on to the stand. The aircraft is being leased from one of our affiliate carriers, which is based in the diamond-rich republic of Yakutiya (Far Eastern Siberia), where, coincidentally, today's shipment of millions has come from.

While we now have an abundance of gems, there doesn't seem to be much sign of any security staff to escort our precious cargo on its short journey to Customs. Before we are able to off-load the baggage, mail and remaining cargo, we need to remove the diamonds from the hold. Unfortunately, without the necessary security back-up we cannot proceed. Shouting over the radio above the noise of passing aircraft, I call base: 'Pat – from Jeremy. Can we give the security company a call to find out where its men are? Perhaps Sharon or Andy in cargo know something?'

Sitting waiting for Pat to call me back, I try to work out how we can move the diamonds ourselves, without jeopardizing our insurance cover. If I reverse my car up to the side of the aircraft and open the boot, it might be misconstrued by somebody, so I quickly abandon that idea. Not having won the National Lottery recently – and therefore not being in a position to welcome instant dismissal – I decide that this is definitely one of those situations that needs to be played exactly by the book.

The sound of cogs turning inside my head is interrupted by Pat's voice: 'Jeremy, the security company say that the guards left their base at least fifteen minutes ago and should already be with you.' As I'm sure I've already mentioned, people have this habit of saying that they – or others – are on their way, but this time I need the truth. If the security guards take much longer to turn up, the loading of the out-going cargo, baggage and mail will be delayed.

Just under forty minutes later, a group of security personnel arrives to transport our precious cargo away from the aircraft and thus allow us to repatriate our arriving passengers with their baggage. We are now left with just forty-two minutes to finish preparing our Airbus A310 for its departure to Tokyo via Moscow. Pat is already at the boarding gate dealing with the passengers and I am on the ramp adjacent to the aircraft, monitoring the staff and ensuring that we are doing our best to meet the 11.00 departure time. Owen, the ramp team leader, has done us proud. By 10.33 he and his team have cleared the hold and are already juggling the out-going containers into position.

Things appear to be coming together nicely, so I park my car back under the terminal and head for the office via the departure gate. Coming up the stairs towards Pat, I can see Mrs Zaitsaeva, who, I must confess, is looking slightly more organized than yesterday. Leastways, her hair appears to be suitably coiffured and she no longer has a soap-on-a-rope round her neck! 'Hello, Mr Spake,' she greets me. 'As you can see, I have managed to arrive in time today. I'm sorry for all the trouble I caused you yesterday.' You've doubtless realized by now that I'm rarely lost for words, but on this occasion I cannot think of anything to say other than, 'Mrs Zaitsaeva, have a pleasant journey!' Apologizing once again, she walks off down the jetty towards the aircraft.

Passing through the double doors into the departure gate, I can see Pat in the distance looking at her watch. 'Everything all right, Patsy?' I ask, conscious that the sands of time are rapidly running out for her. 'Sweetness,' she replies, 'if you're going back to the office, could you possibly make a last-call announcement in Russian on your way?' Pat then informs me that she's still thirty or so punters missing. With this in mind, I walk as quickly as possible towards the info desk.

'Excuse me. Are you that bloke that's been on telly?' comes the somewhat excited voice of a man in his late twenties who's dragging a small suitcase on wheels and running towards me with a mobile telephone clamped to his ear. 'Yes, I am, sir,' I own up. 'What can I do for you?' Addressing someone at the other end of his phone, he says, 'You're never going to believe this, Rob. Guess who's stood next to me – that guy from Aeroflot. You know, the one that speaks Russian who was in that *Airport* show.'

Clearly, Rob is in some doubt about what the traveller is talking about because the mobile is suddenly pushed into my face: 'Go on – tell 'im who you are, mate!' Sometimes it's really hard to cope with instant fame and recognition! Right now, I need to make an urgent announcement for Aunty Pat, but instead I'm speaking on a mobile to some stranger. 'Hi there!' I say. 'I'm Jeremy from Aeroflot.'

Clearly, this is not enough and more is needed from the chap at the other end, who suddenly asks, 'Say something in Russian to me, then.' Not wanting to disappoint his friend, who's breathing down my neck, I offer several greetings in Russian and pass the mobile back to the excited passenger. 'Thanks, mate,' he mutters, 'that's amazing. I never thought I'd see you in real life. Thanks, that's really great!'

Duty done, I proceed across the concourse hoping to rout out our missing passengers by means of an announcement. The information desk already has a large crowd around it, with people trying to make contact with lost friends, relatives and business associates. Stepping into the office behind the front counter is like entering a quiet harbour during a force nine gale. This is one of the few places in the airport where it's possible to catch your breath and have a bit of a chuckle with the hard-pressed staff. The people who work at information desks in the airport are the public face of Heathrow, and as such have to put up with an awful lot of abuse. Personally, I have every admiration for them. *'Vnimani vnimaniye, vsye...'* Having made the all-important last-call announcement in Russian, I'm delighted to hear Patsy saying on the radio, 'Complete 581.' So everyone's on board, and it's just 11.02!

Bidding my information-desk colleagues farewell, I head back across the terminal towards the warren of corridors and the office. 'Sorry, mate! D'you mind if I take a picture of you? I'm sure Rob didn't believe me.'

Yes, you've guessed, it's our mobile-clutching friend who's been patiently awaiting my return so that he can grab some vital photographic evidence for his office. While I oblige, I spot Igor, who seems to be smirking, coming towards me. *'Zdrasvoi Gor, no kak ti?'* Having informed me, with a smile on his face, that all is well, Igor says he will wait for me while I have my photo taken.

To be perfectly honest, I've no idea why Igor is smiling so much. Friday is his paperwork day and he normally arrives like a bear with a sore head. 'What's so funny, Gor?' I enquire, expecting some sarcastic retort. 'I'm just very pleased to see, my dear Mr General Secretary, that you are posing for your subjects!' At this point, we are joined by Comrade Commissar Dave Thomashenko from Czech Airlines.

There are very few occasions when I feel incapable of controlling a situation, but when Igor and Dave get together, it is torture. As we make our way back through the maze of corridors, accompanied as usual by the feeling that we are trying to dig ourselves out from something equivalent to *The Great Escape*, I'm subjected to continuous comments concerning PC – Party Correctness – and how I should lead by example. Because I'm conserving my energy for later in the day, I decide not to take the bait and inform Dave that I will try to see him later for coffee.

11:30 Kasia returns to the office looking whacked. '*Krasarvitsa maiya*, have you been busy down there on the ticket desk?' Before our very own Polish Empress opens her mouth to reply to my question, she throws down an enormous envelope full of money. Trying not to crack her freshly applied layer of lip gloss, she informs me, 'Honestly, it's been really busy. I've been run off my feet! You can't imagine how many people – it seemed as though the queue was never going to go away!'

The sight of so much money is beginning to worry me. Perhaps she has carried out our threat and transformed our 'Show Case' into a kiosk without a trader's licence! What will the bods at the BAA say about that? (BAA are the owners of Heathrow Airport Limited.) 'Kashinka,' I venture, 'have you been selling bread again?' My aristocratic colleague laughs as Pat places a cup of lemon tea for her on the table. 'I know,' I add, 'you've been offering beauty therapy treatments to our passengers. How many manicures did you manage to get through?'

I'm cheated from any response by the sight of the second flight of the day entering the zone. '241 zoning for Fox 10 everyone,' I declare, picking up my freshly re-charged radio and high-visibility jacket, ready to do battle once again at the departure gate.

Pat leaves the office with me and we head for check-in together. On our way downstairs, she briefs me about tonight's duties in West Drayton. 'Jeremy, don't forget that the five black kittens will need to be kept in tonight.' Suddenly, the prospect of cat-sitting doesn't seem so appealing. I had completely forgotten that Patsy was currently fostering five demanding little kittens. Keeping an eye on them will be truly arduous and the evening will not be as relaxing as I had hoped.

My first port of call at check-in is the First/Business Class desk, where there's a shabbily dressed passenger demanding to see the Aeroflot supervisor. 'That's me, sir. How can I help you?' Proving yet again that you really can't tell a book by its cover, I discover, as I try to assist the rather irate American, that he is holding an open-dated First Class ticket. 'This girl here,' states our transatlantic cousin, pointing in the general direction of Ms Brown behind the counter, 'informs me there's no First Class cabin on this aircraft. I bought me a First Class ticket. What you gonna do about it? No one told me there won't be no First Class.' Just my luck! This afternoon's flight is being operated by one of our Boeing 767-300 aircraft, which is capable of carrying only 226 passengers in a two-class configuration, Business and Economy, or should I say Coach Class, this being the term Americans use for Economy Class.

American passengers can be notoriously difficult to please, so if I am going to avoid an ear-lashing, my line of questioning will need to be delicate. 'I note you have an open ticket, sir. Did you or your travel agent make a reservation for today's flight?' 'Look, boy, my travel agent in Charlotte, North Carolina, told me I don't need no reservation. I just gotta bring myself to the counter and get on that there plane!'

Hearing this not uncommon response is like a red rag to a bull as far as I am concerned. It's bad enough when people hold a reservation and fail to turn up to travel, but it's simply too much when someone arrives without a booking and is then amazed to discover that a seat is not available, or that the class of travel they desire is full.

'I'm terribly sorry, sir, but today we're operating an American-built Boeing 767 and this aircraft is only equipped to fly Business and Economy Class. It normally operates to New York every day and we have found that there is very little demand for First Class from America.' Yes, I am trying to win ground by implying that perhaps his problem stems from his fellow compatriots and not from the Russians, who I'm certain are about to get the blame. 'If someone had phoned to reserve a seat for you, sir, we would have been able to advise them of this fact. But, right now, we have a seat for you only in Business Class. Naturally, you'll be given access to the First Class lounge!'

Fortunately, my dear friend Ms Brown has already had a similar conversation with the passenger, and victory on this occasion appears to be ours as he reluctantly states, 'Okay, boy, I'll travel Business Class, but I'm not happy.' Not surprisingly, he continues to ram this point home, but I gently remind him that it is always advisable to call the airline before setting out for the airport.

Watching the now Business Class passenger wandering off with a trolley full of VAT reclaim baggage, I catch sight of Aunty Pat. She's busy debating the finer points of packing 20 kilos of baggage with one of the seven transit passengers we are expecting today via Moscow to Ghana. Yes, it's that old chestnut again – excess! Thankfully, though, Pat is more than capable of convincing the passenger that he has too much baggage and I leave the debate in her safe hands.

Making my merry way towards the pier (no, not Brighton – Terminal 2, which has two main piers from where flights depart), in the general direction of Gate 10, I catch a glimpse of another of my many Russian friends, who's just about to pass through Immigration, having arrived on our in-bound flight. 'Tonya, I had no idea you were coming over. How's life treating you?'

After a brief chat in Russian, I learn that Tonya – another of my academically endowed friends, who's from Yaroslavl, just north of Moscow – has arrived to teach alongside Natasha. Thankfully, some-one from the university is waiting in arrivals to whisk her away to Colchester. 'Tonya, it's such a pleasure to see you again. It must be all of a year since we were last together. I'll be on campus next week, so we'll be able to catch up with each other then. Natash has already

 'One of our aeroplanes is missing.' Parking stand Echo 40 is visible in the distance, but there's no sign of an Aeroflot plane. Only British Midland has managed to find some takers. Looks like I can knock off early for a change.

settled into the university routine and we're planning to go for good old fish and chips on Monday, so you'll have to join us. Okay?' Tonya confirms in true Russian style that meeting on Monday would be convenient and then kisses me goodbye. She knows how busy I am and clearly doesn't want to delay me any longer.

Passing the windows that look out across the ramp, I can see our aircraft shining in the sun. This particular 767 represents a coup for the American manufac-  turer, as it was the first-ever American-built aircraft to enter the Aeroflot fleet. Since its arrival, we have seen the introduction of other Boeing types in the shape of 737s and the latest 777.

On board, the cleaners are busy tidying the cabin, while the crew are checking safety equipment and counting the return catering supplies. Down on the ramp, standing next to the nose wheel, is Michael, the Delta Airlines' engineer, who is responsible for our line maintenance when 767s come to London. Michael lived in Moscow for a few years, training our own engineering staff, so he speaks a little Russian. Right now, though, he's chatting in English with the First Officer, who is walking round the Boeing carrying out routine visual checks. 'Hi, Michael. How's things, mate?' All's well, he tells me, with him and his family, and the aircraft is fine, too. Leaving Michael to supervise the loading of the fuel, I make my way upstairs to brief the crew.

As we rarely see the Boeing 767 in London nowadays, the crew are unfamiliar to me. They are, however, a cheery young bunch, with a chief stewardess who appears to have all the efficiency of our Colonel Kleb, but who likes to talk. Although I am almost dead on my feet, I am encouraged by the pleasantry of my flying friends and decide to engage in a bit of general chit-chat before asking, 'Has Boris Nikolaevich given you the passenger figures yet?' 'Yes, he has. I believe we are expecting 31 business and 183 economy passengers. Is that right?' Unable to fault the crew member's memory, we agree a time of 13.05 for boarding and I leave them to enjoy their lunch in peace.

The 767 is equipped with two large holds divided into four compartments under the floor of the main passenger cabin. This area provides us with exceptional freight-carrying capacity. My colleagues in cargo have been busy selling the available space all week, and we are expecting nearly 7.5 tons of goods that have been packed on to three specialist metal pallets for ease of loading.

Walking up the jetty towards the departure gate, I happen to glance through one of the windows, which are reminiscent of ships' portholes. Wait a second! The men on the ramp look as though they've got nothing to do. Now, any of you who have sat in a departure lounge looking out of the window while your flight is being loaded cannot fail to have noticed how frantic things can be. Trucks and men everywhere busily trying to meet a deadline. So why are my staff standing around idle? Abandoning the gate for a few minutes, I pop downstairs on to the ramp again. 'Mark, mate! What's up? Are you waiting for baggage to be delivered from the terminal?' Mark, the ramp team leader, responds, 'It's not the baggage, Jeremy, mate – most of that's here already with the mail. We're waiting for the bloody cargo to arrive. Some prick must have cocked up somewhere!'

Honest, the ramp can be quite a refreshing place at times! While the language might offend some people, no one can deny that the guys who load the aircraft are anything other than brutally honest during a crisis! All I ever want to hear are the facts, so Mark wins my vote every time. After all, trying to make things sound better than they are is no good – not in the airline game! 'Okay, Mark,' I say, 'I'll get on to cargo and find out what the hell's happening. In the meantime, you'll need to check with the dispatcher as I want you to start loading the stuff that's already here, please.'

Leaving Mark to confirm with the dispatcher where to position the containers that are to hand, I go to phone my colleague Sharon in cargo. Sharon's office is situated on the south side of the airport, so visiting her is not a practical option. 'Sharon, it's me, hon! What's happening with today's shipments?'

Sharon, who is every bit as down to earth as yours truly, can sense the urgency in my voice, but regretfully has to inform me, 'They've only just finished building the freight, so it should be leaving here in about five minutes. One of the shipments was delivered late to the sheds this morning, so it's taken longer to process everything. I'll give you a shout on the radio when the trucks leave for the aircraft.'

I should add that cargo is processed in a similar manner to passengers. A document known as an Airway Bill (a bit like a passenger ticket) has to be issued before any freight can be accepted. The consignee then delivers the freight to our warehouse, where it is registered on the computer system, security-screened and then loaded into or on to specialist equipment for transportation.

Looking at my watch, I see it's already 12.57, time to catch up with the staff at the gate. Life really is amazing at Heathrow, you know! It's

✈ OVERLEAF 'Hello, are you keeping that Teletubby nice and warm there under your coat?' Me greeting one of our many young Russian travellers. This particular young lady was the last to arrive at the gate, but I couldn't possibly be angry with her.

almost as if the passengers can sense that I've got a few problems with cargo and are on their very best behaviour. As I look around the gate area, I'm astonished to see that a large proportion of today's travellers have already arrived for boarding. Resisting the temptation to pinch myself – just to confirm I really am awake – I go to the front desk and say, 'Don't tell me – we're only a few passengers missing.'

All four of the AFSL boarding team turn and look at me. Simon, the assistant passenger supervisor, says, 'Jeremy, you're never going to believe this … ' 'No, I don't suppose for one minute I will, Simon!' 'Well, we're only missing three passengers and we know exactly where they are!' *'Kak ne mozhet byt!'* At times like this, I often break into Russian, forgetting that the AFSL staff won't comprehend my utterings. 'It's a conspiracy everyone,' I chortle. 'This has to be a first! With twenty-six minutes left before departure at 1.30, you're telling me that only three passengers haven't arrived. Please don't think I'm accusing you of trying to pull the wool over my eyes, but I can't believe it!'

Overwhelmed, I start to make the boarding announcements, but, as always, the radio starts hissing. 'Gate – from Cargo.' 'Yeah, go ahead, Sharon.' 'Jeremy, the trucks are just leaving and should be with you no later than twenty-past.'

Passengers start filing past me as I begin to assess the situation. Theory tells me that we should be able to load the three pallets in a quarter of an hour, which will mean a take-off delay of just five minutes. Five minutes, while not desirable, is, under the circumstances, acceptable.

 'Sharon – from Jeremy. There's no sign of the freight, love! Are you certain it's on its way? I can't afford to wait much longer.' 'Stand by,' my buxom buddy from Cargo informs me, 'I'll just double-check with the staff downstairs.'

An eternity seems to pass while I stand on the ramp with the loaders eagerly awaiting news. After just two minutes Sharon is back on the radio to inform me that the trucks were unable to pass through the cargo tunnel because the freight had slipped sideways on the pallets and was now overhanging the sides, thus causing a possible safety hazard to on-coming vehicles. 'Jeremy,' she adds, 'the trucks are now having to be escorted across the live taxi-ways.' This, quite frankly, is news I could do without. Peering into the distance, I can see the trucks waiting on the other side of the runway for a departing aircraft to pass them.

Picture the situation. Flight SU242 should have departed three minutes ago, all 214 passengers are sitting comfortably in their seats, the baggage and mail are loaded, but there's still no cargo. And because all our weekend cargo capacity has been booked, I'm committed to having to wait for the lorries to arrive.

Over the noise of a passing United Airlines' Boeing 777, Mark shouts, 'Look over there, Jeremy. One of the trucks has got smoke coming from it!' Really, this is getting to be beyond a joke. I've waited over an hour for these blasted shipments to come to the aircraft, and now, just within sight, they're about to go up in a puff of smoke! Turning to Mark, I say, 'I can't bear to watch. The captain's already barking at us to get this show on the road and I don't think I've got the stomach to tell him that the wait has been in vain because there ain't going to be no cargo.'

Finally, at 13.44, the trucks arrive alongside the aircraft with their cargo intact. Seemingly, one of the drivers was experiencing engine overheat and the breeze across the runway was making things look much worse than they really were. Good, we're now in a position to load the pallets and, hopefully, should be away on the hour at 2 p.m.

Mark and his team position the first two pallets on the high-lifter crane and slide them up into the aircraft. While two of the men are inside the hold securing the pallets and containers down with special locking pins, Mark is desperately trying to get the final pallet through the door. I sense a problem! 'Now what, Mark? I don't think I can take much more of this.'

Cast your mind back, reader, to when the lorries were unable to come via the normal route through the tunnel. On that occasion, somebody said that the freight had slipped sideways on the pallet and was overhanging the side of the truck. Well, that, we are now discovering, was true. The last pallet, no matter how much we jiggle it about, is not going to go on the aircraft. 'Mark, forget it, mate. Just take the damn thing off. We've wasted enough time already.' The bedraggled team-leader needs no further instruction. Before we have time to count to twenty, the men are clear of the aircraft and the captain is busy talking to Michael through his headset.

Clearance is given to push back at 14.02, and as I wave them off from the ramp, the captain gives me a friendly know-what-you've-been-through smile from the cockpit window. After all the excitement I need to let off steam and take a long walk back to the office. Strolling along, I think of that saying, 'Never work with children or animals.' After today, I've decided to add cargo to this list.

 Bliss. The world of Aeroflot Heathrow has fallen silent for another day. Kasia finished her shift at 4 p.m. and Patsy has gone off to put on her glad rags for tonight's dinner party. Because I'm still fighting a losing battle with my paperwork, I've agreed with Pat that I will be at her place around 7 p.m., just in time to run through the final cat-watch briefing before she and Adrian leave for the jollities.

Just as I start to see the top of my desk for the first time in a week, there's a knock at the door. I'm faced with the difficult decision of whether or not to open it. There could, after all, be a passenger on the other side wanting to grab me by the jugular for some reason or another, especially after the kind of day I've just had.

Oh, what the hell? In for a penny, in a pound, as they say. Throwing caution to the wind, I open the door and am delighted to see Comrade Dave, Heathrow's longest-serving airline station manager. 'I've had water in my kettle all day and been eagerly awaiting an audience with your General Secretaryness. Where've you been?' Offering my humble apologies, I invite my old mate into the office to partake of our drinking facilities.

'This isn't just a social call,' Comrade Dave says. 'I've come to remind you about tomorrow night.' Looking over the top of my glasses for that all-important General Secretary effect, I tell my loyal subject, 'Thomashenko, do you doubt the General Secretary's memory capacity? Do you not realize that such thoughts are punishable – that it's never too late to check out the hospitality of the local gulags!'

✈ Unlike Pat and Kasia, my part of the office is neat and tidy, being watched over by V.I. Lenin and Brezhnev's personal pilot. I'm very smug in the knowledge that I know the exact whereabouts of everything I need!

Dave still looks doubtful. Have I remembered, he repeats, that he is having a bit of a get-together at his house tomorrow night? Of course, I have. I'm just not sure whether I'll be able to make it. Saturday is Day Six of my shift and my energy is already sapping at an enormous rate. Fortunately, because Dave has been in the industry for more years than I care to think about, he understands that I'm on the edge of losing my sanity and knows that I will do my best to attend his get-together if I can.

On the wall opposite my desk are two clocks. The top one is set for Moscow's local time, and the lower one displays GMT. Incidentally, the airline industry bases its aircraft movement messages entirely upon the Greenwich Meridian. Right now, given the time difference, it's 21.30 in Russia's capital and in England, time for me to make my way to West Drayton's very own cat paradise.

Pulling up outside Pat's house, just eight minutes after leaving the madness of the airport, is like drinking a large glass of neat, ice-cold vodka. Wonderful. On the drive to Pat's, I've not witnessed a single driver gesticulating through the windscreen of his car, or hurling abuse through an open window. While I love living in the rural world of Colchester, it's very nice occasionally to be able to avoid all the road-rage traumas happening on Britain's motorways and main roads. The entrance to number four swings open and there, standing in the doorway, is my dear old Aunty Pat, looking stunning in her evening wear. 'Patsy, you look lovely.' Without wasting any time, Pat reminds me that I know where everything is and leaves with Adrian for her dinner party.

21:45 After a couple of hours watching telly, cooking something to eat and single-handedly re-enacting the feeding of the 5000 – well, all right, then, fifteen or so assorted moggies, I'm completely shattered and decide to hit the stairs for bed. Just as I begin my weary way up, I remember that I need to check that the five almost identical black kittens are safely locked in for the night.

There's me been thinking all these years that counting humans on to aircraft is difficult… Believe me, trying to keep track of five squirmy perishers is a great deal more troublesome. 'One, two…eight …' No, that can't be right… Pat definitely said there were only five. Start again. Panic begins to set in. My cat-loving colleague will never forgive me if I lose one of 'em.

More than twenty minutes later – when I'm developing black spots before my eyes – I admit defeat and go to bed for some well-earned rest. Today has been eventful and interesting to say the very least, but its various highs and lows do not even enter my thoughts as I drop off to sleep. All I can think about is a small black kitten, lost, mewing pitifully and wandering the streets of West Drayton. This really is the stuff that nightmares are made of!

✈ Cat-sitting at Pat's house, surrounded by her pussies!

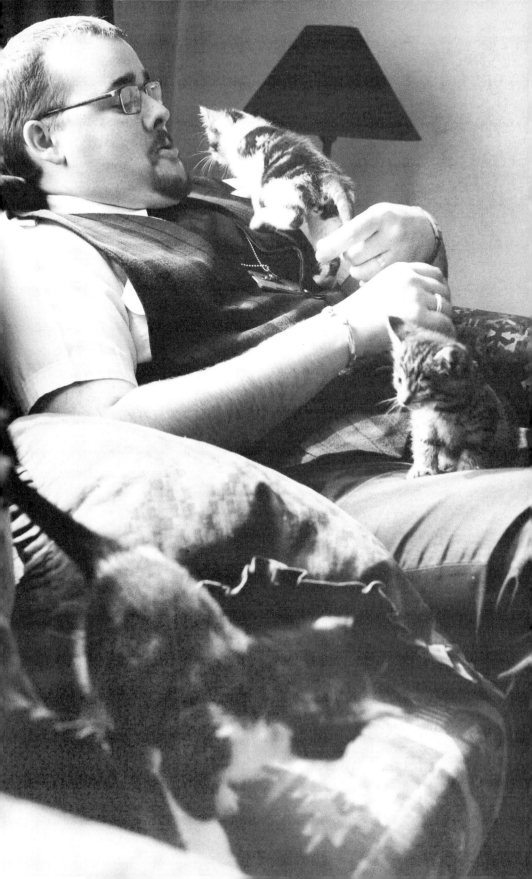

CHAPTER 6

SURVIVAL OF THE FITTEST

SATURDAY

THE NIGHTMARE'S A REALITY! After a very bad sleep filled with images of destitute felines wandering the wilds of West Drayton without a scrap to eat, I'm rudely awakened by a dawn chorus of starving moggies. As I stretch across to look at the clock, the cats begin to attack my feet, thinking it's flesh for the taking. 'Get off you lot. Behave yourselves. What are you like! I'll feed you all in a minute!' Bless 'em! It's 6.11 a.m. precisely. Boy, am I glad I didn't waste any energy setting the alarm clock last night!

'Come on you lot, get off. Then, I'll come down and feed you.' As the cats jump off the bed and head towards the door, last night's incorrect head-count comes rushing back to me. At least one of our cats is missing, and in less than two hours I'm going to have to face Aunty Pat with the bad news.

My head begins to fill with thoughts of Shakespeare's *Macbeth*. Crystal-clear images of Pat standing over a large black cauldron, with Kasia and Gabi at her side, take on an alarmingly lifelike three-witches feel. Do you ever get to the point where you start to hear voices? No? Well, I do: 'Double, double,

----

Nearing the end of a busy week, I take a few quiet moments to reflect on all that has happened.

toil and trouble, cauldron boil and Jeremy bubble.' Help! Give me missing passengers any day – at least there are procedures in place for dealing with that.

Hot on the heels of my extended feline family, I go down to the living-room to begin the arduous task of re-counting the little beggars. *Raz, dva, tri … vosem …* Blast! Even when I count in Russian, I seem to end up with eight *chornikh koshek* (black kittens). It's no good, I'm going to have to try and corner them all in the kitchen, where there's no escape. Only one small snag – Pat forgot to mention that they all seem terrified of coming too close to humans. I know how they feel! Okay, I'll open a packet of prime ham – that'll have 'em rushing to me. Wrong! They're far too clever for that little trick. Obviously my cat-loving colleague's tried that one before. Thanks a bunch, Patsy!

How, I wonder, does David Attenborough manage to get up so close to wild animals? Maybe, to discover his secret, I should volunteer to participate in BBC1's wildlife programmes rather than fly-on-wall documentaries! After twenty or so minutes of wrestling with kittens on the floor of the kitchen, I decide to give up the head-count and go for a shower. Upstairs, there are moggies everywhere. I begin to feel someone is re-making Hitchcock's famous *Birds* movie, but this time starring cats, without the assistance of Andrew Lloyd Webber.

My hoped-for peaceful night has turned out to be one of the most traumatic experiences of my short life. In between showering and breakfast (yes, you're quite correct, I don't normally have breakfast, but this is comfort-eating, you understand) I've attempted to count my charges at least fifteen times and still cannot make the numbers tally. If the last twelve hours are any indication of what I might expect over the remainder of my shift, I'd better give up here and now.

With a look of utter remorse-cum-terror on my face, I close the door to number four and walk to the car. The moment when I will have to face the music is fast approaching. Time can be a very cruel animal – no pun intended – when it wants! Turning the key in the ignition, I glance back at the house and see some of the cats silhouetted in an upstairs window. Believe me, this image will haunt me for the remainder of the day, if not the entire shift – or my life!

Entering the all but deserted tunnel into the central area of the airport, I draw up alongside Pat, who, sitting in her usual semi-slumped position behind the wheel, sees me and beams. Oh, no! A sinking feeling washes over me as I grin half-heartedly back through the passenger window of my car. Fortunately, I need to pass through one of those famous CPs in order to have my car airside for today's busy schedule. (Yes, this is the part of the book where you would normally have to turn back several chapters to discover what on earth CP stands for, but because I have the welfare of everyone in mind, I'll save you the bother: CP stands for Control Post, remember?) Doing this, means I'll have a few extra moments to dream up a worthy excuse for having mislaid a kitten or two!

Minty (my black VW Polo) doesn't know what's happening to her this morning. Being so used to the long drive from Colchester, she seems to sigh with relief as I park in my usual spot, just eleven minutes after setting off. My brain is already working overtime trying to conjure up, but failing to think of, a remotely plausible missing-kitten excuse. Forlorn, I decide to dice with death and go via the Tardis to the office. With luck, this technologically advanced (suicide) capsule will jam again and I'll expire from a lack of oxygen and never be required to own up to the awful truth about the goings-on at number four last night. But no, my hopes are dashed as the glass sarcophagus lets out a pneumatic hiss and the door swings open.

Gingerly entering the office, I catch sight of Pat busy reading and tearing up in-coming telexes, while telling Igor, Harry and Kasia the wonders of her evening out. Before I've even had a chance to wish everyone a pleasant morning, she confronts me with, 'Morning, sweet. Did you have a good evening – are all the cats okay?' Although Pat has already sensed that something's wrong, I spend the next ten minutes rambling on like Magnus Pike, trying to avoid answering any of her questions.

In fact, to delay the inevitable and throw her off the scent, I decide to ask a few questions myself: 'Has St Petersburg sent confirmation that the stretcher's been fitted into the passenger cabin?' As Aunty Pat passes me the relevant telex, her expression tells me my ploy hasn't worked. While I pretend to read the message, she questions me again in a tone of voice reminiscent of the three witches. 'Is something wrong, Jeremy? You don't seem your usual self this morning.' It's no good – I admit defeat and tell the whole sorry tale of woe.

Thankfully, it transpires that Patsy frequently had the same trouble keeping track of the little beasties when she first got them, and that it is only after much trial and error that she's able to account for each and every one of them every night. Phew! I will, after all, be going home in one piece today.

Recovering from the initial trauma of the morning, I'm now able to turn my thoughts to the business at hand and once again read the telex concerning the dreaded stretcher. 'Gorskii,' I say to Igor, who is sat in front of the computer reading all the messages, 'have you seen the telex from Pulkovo about the stretcher? I don't believe it, do you?' Igor has clearly seen that our colleagues in St Petersburg have failed to fit the stretcher into the cabin as promised. Somebody in sales control has allowed all the Business Class seats on the in-bound flight to be sold, which means that the engineers cannot fit the specialist equipment. 'Yeah, Jemskii, I read it! I can't believe it either. Those charming little Burgers want us to fit it here!'

What, I hear you ask, is difficult about that? Well, the stretcher needs to be bolted securely on to the frames of at least four Business Class seats, a process that neither Igor nor myself are familiar with. In true Russian style, we decide not to let this little hitch stand in our way and vow to face the challenge head on. Sure, we might have a slight delay, but by hook or by crook we'll get the stretcher fitted and the passenger will travel.

Saturday is a particularly busy day in the world of Aeroflot Heathrow. We have two flights to Moscow, one to St Petersburg and a night-stopping aircraft arriving from Tokyo and Moscow. Incidentally, I should mention that the St Petersburg flight is operated under a franchise agreement by Pulkovo Air Enterprises. Taking a close look at the report prepared by Kasia, I see that the three departing flights will generate nearly 640 passengers and that one of these is the Russian Ambassador to the United Kingdom. Each of us is going to need all the strength we can muster to survive the next eight or so hours.

Flight SU247, an Ilyushin IL86, is due to land in a little over an hour. The first out-bound flight of the day, logically known as SU248, is at 11 a.m., and check-in started on time at 8 o'clock.

'Aeroflot base – from check-in.' Hello! What a shock! Someone from AFSL has managed to locate us on the Aeroflot radio. We *really* must do a better job of hiding that! Summing up the energy, I respond, 'Go ahead, Alex.' 'Morning, Jeremy. Is one of you coming down to check-in? We have a few excess baggage problems.'

I can't put it off any longer. It's time for me to make my presence felt. Leaving my coffee to go cold, I pick up my radio and a copy of Kashinka's handiwork (the daily report) and head out of the office with Patsy, who, by the way, is still grinning like a Cheshire cat. It's unnerving! If I didn't know better, I could be forgiven for thinking that the people in our office had been prescribed happy pills. Igor smirked all day yesterday and now Pat's at it, even though she's about to staff the ticket desk. I tell you, it's unnatural!

As we break out into the open space of the concourse from one of the many corridors, it's immediately apparent that we are facing a bigger problem in terms of people than Thursday. The queue for Central Search is stretching the entire length of the building, and is already starting to encroach on to the ramp that leads to Terminal 1. 'Patsy, just take a look at that!' I say. 'It's unbelievable. Where are they all coming from?' At last, the grin on Patsy's face begins to fade as the impact of seeing so many punters hits her. 'Pat,' I mutter, 'my name's Michael Caine and that there queue is the entire Zulu army!' Without hesitation, Pat wittily retorts, 'I know! Not so long ago, there was some talk about re-naming Heathrow, but I had no idea they'd decided to name it Rorke's Drift!'

The sheer number of people means that there's no easy route to the ground floor, so Pat and I give in gracefully and join the hordes heading for check-in. Just as we reach the top of the stairs, there's a commotion taking place between a group of passengers. 'Good God, man! What the hell are you trying to do – kill us all?' booms the voice of an aristocratic-looking Englishman in his early sixties.

'Can you see what's going on over there, Jeremy?' Pat asks. Peering over the top of a rather large lady with too much baggage, I attempt to respond to the question. 'Difficult to say, love, but it looks like some bloke is trying to go *down* the *up* escalator with a trolley full of baggage.'

Sure enough, one man doesn't seem to have grasped the fact that the escalators are for up only, and that if he wishes to go down, he needs to use the lift! On this occasion, I can see that there's no need for me to do my Sir Lancelot act, as the Englishman has grabbed hold of the offending trolley and is dragging it, owner attached, towards the lifts.

We finally make it in one piece to the ground floor, where the air conditioning is struggling to cope with the pressure of so many hot sweaty bodies pressed together. To be frank, my immediate impression is that the United Nations has transferred its headquarters from New York to Terminal 2. Blood pressures appear to be on the boil, and we seem to have the A to Z of the human spectrum, from Austrians to Zambians, all fighting to get to the front of a queue. Suddenly, I realize why Pat was smiling so much. Being tucked away on the ticket desk, far from the madding crowd, means her morning is going to be relatively stress free.

 Baggage, baggage and, by way of a change, yet more baggage! We've got seven desks open and every single member of staff is working flat out to try and clear the horrendous queues.

'Jeremy!' 'Yes, Alex? What's wrong now?' Alex, who has been given the unenviable task of queue combing (making sure that passengers are

---

✈ Making a quick exit from an irate passenger down the unique integral steps of one of our Ilyushin IL86s. Damn handy these, especially when the crew and passengers are champing at the bit to get airborne!

in the right queue for their particular ticket), is beginning to foam at the mouth with the stress of it all, as he summons me over to chat with a group of Russians who seem determined to take all their baggage as hand-luggage into the cabin with them.

The thing to remember at this point, reader, is that on some domestic flights in Russia operated by Ilyushin IL86 aircraft, passengers carry their own baggage as far as the plane, where it is then loaded on to special racks under the main cabin floor. The people in front of me, who know that the aircraft they are about to fly on is an IL86, have barely understood a word that Alex has said and have assumed that they will be taking their luggage with them. *'Izvinite ... vy predstavitel Aeroflota?'* enquires the group leader. Answering in Russian, I say, 'Yes, sir, I'm the Aeroflot representative. What can I do for you?' After yet another ten-minute discussion, I manage to persuade the group that they need to check their baggage in and then wave goodbye to it as it passes along the conveyor belt for loading.

Check-in now resembles an Egyptian flea market with all the different airline staff being subjected to passengers desperately trying to haggle away any excess baggage charges. I've had my fair share of negotiations, which is evident from the steam rising from Pat's pen over on the ticket desk as she frantically issues excess baggage tickets. Above the noise of excited voices comes the regal and somewhat calming tone of Kashinka on the radio: '247 landed about ten minutes ago, guys, and is parked on Golf 12.' Kasia then confirms that she will be at check-in shortly to relieve me so that I can make my more-than-weary way to the gate.

Leaving Kasia to do battle with the ever-growing crowds at check-in, I pass through the Staff Central Search area, which is already like a greenhouse, and begin to wish I had invested in a pair of uniform shorts. But entering our Ilyushin IL86 aircraft, a pleasant on-board breeze hits me. At last, a chance to cool down. Igor is busy discussing technical issues with the flight engineer, so I leave him in peace and head off down the cabin to check how the cleaners are getting on. Catching sight of the eight-strong team, I call to the supervisor, 'Hi, there! Another ten minutes is all I can give you, guys. Okay?'

That done, it's time to brief the cabin crew about today's load.

Approaching the first-class compartment of this mighty aircraft, I greet the cabin chief, who's a regular visitor to London and a personal favourite of mine: *'No privyet! Kak ty?'* 'Jeremy, *please!'* she replies. 'You know I want to practise my English skills, so let's discuss these matters in Queen Elizabeth's language. Thank you!' It's always a pleasure to help my Moscow colleagues, so I oblige by finishing my brief in English. 'Oh, and by the way, the Russian Ambassador's travelling on this flight. He should be sat in 1A, with his wife next to him in 1B.'

Just as the Chief Stewardess is repeating the passenger numbers to me in near-perfect English, the cleaning supervisor comes up. 'Jeremy, one of the rear toilets is blocked and there's water everywhere.' *'Please,'* I retort, 'we don't need this right now! How bad is it?' While this may seem a daft question, the cleaning supervisor knows that I need to weigh up the situation and assess any possibility of delay. 'To be honest,' she replies, 'I think you'd better come and look. As I said, the water's everywhere!'

Regretfully, she's not exaggerating. Some really considerate passenger (yes, sarcasm is intended) on the inward flight has shoved enough toilet roll down the pan to keep a small sewage farm fully occupied for days. What possesses these people, bless 'em? 'Okay,' I say to the supervisor, 'if we can mop up some of the water on the floor, I'll get the engineer to try and unblock the toilet. You'll also need to get that sucker machine thingy on to the carpet.'

In addition to the blocked toilet, the cleaning crew have also discovered that seat 28B has had coffee spilt all over it and cannot therefore be used. I now need to move the passenger who's been allocated this spot to another place. It never rains but it pours!

Resigning myself to the fact that the cabin's beginning to look like one of those fish tanks you see in Chinese restaurants, I make my way up to the departure gate to see the staff and to arrange for the passenger in seat 28B to be moved. 'How's things here, everyone?' I ask, adding: 'Blimey, it's a bit like the *Marie Celeste* at the moment. Where

✈ OVERLEAF 'You're not available at the weekend, are you love? My pad could do with a good spring clean!' I find a few minutes during the short turnaround to pass the time of day with one of the cleaning staff.

are all the passengers?' Smiling, the boarding team leader replies, 'We're all fine, thanks, Jeremy. I've just announced the flight, so the passengers should start arriving in a few minutes.' 'Brilliant! Can we have a look in the system to see who's sat in 28B? There's been an accident and we need to block the seat off.'

Before the team leader's had a chance to respond to my question, the remaining staff are grimacing and speculating about what kind of catastrophe has befallen seat 28B. Resisting the temptation to let their imaginations run riot, I inform them, 'No, it's not what you think! Someone's spilt their coffee, thank you very much. Behave yourselves! No idleness, please.'

Just my luck! The passenger in 28B is travelling with someone, and there's only one vacant seat left in Economy Class to where I can move the unsuspect-  ing traveller. Now why, I hear you saying, don't I just move the occu- pant of 28B to the remaining seat available and leave his or her companion in 28A? Well, nothing's that simple. I know from experi- ence that if one is moved, the other will want to go too, which in my book (no, not the one you're reading, the book of logic stored in my head) is fair enough. I know this because I still have very vivid memo- ries of about five years ago when I was faced with an almost identical conundrum. Being younger then, and slightly wet behind the ears, I didn't think twice about splitting up two businessmen, who, for company budgetary reasons, were travelling Economy Class.

On being informed that they were to be separated, one of the men broke out in an instant sweat, while the other seemed pleased and, letting out a sigh of relief, scurried off towards the aircraft. 'Is this *really* necessary?' the remaining passenger protested. 'Can't somebody

---

✦ No, this isn't a case of more excess baggage, or an offshoot of a Chinese laundry. This is the cleaning team tidying the aircraft in record quick time for the return flight to Moscow.

✈ OVERLEAF 'It's your turn to tell the passengers that we have an hour's delay.' This will have to be settled by the pistols-at-dawn method. Igor and I discuss some technicalities: we can't afford to miss our take-off slot.

ВЫХОД
EXIT

САЛОН
1 КЛАССА

9 D

else be moved?' 'Unfortunately, sir,' I replied, 'the flight is very busy. I have to move one of you and can't offer to move both of you because that would mean reshuffling the whole of the Economy Class cabin, which, regretfully, isn't practical. I will, however, arrange a free bottle of champagne for both of you to compensate for the inconvenience.'

Without further ado – but still perspiring copiously – the passenger trundled off, leaving me to go about the business of finalizing the flight for departure. Ten minutes later everybody was on board and the aircraft was already being pushed back for departure. There, I thought, satisfied, all's well that ends well! But, even though I was young and inexperienced, I should've have known that things are rarely that simple. Just as the aircraft was about to make its final move towards the end of the runway, I received a garbled message that the flight was 'returning to stand' (the phrase used to describe an aircraft forced to come back to the terminal building – usually for a technical reason).

Frantically trying to ascertain what was wrong, I called various people, but all to no avail. No one seemed certain what the problem was. Perhaps, we were left speculating, the captain had detected a technical fault?

The mystery, however, was instantly resolved when the door of the Boeing 737-500 was opened. The passenger who had earlier protested about being separated from his colleague had turned out to be somebody who was terrified of flying. For fifteen years he had relied on his colleague to get him through business flights, and this was the first time he had been faced with the prospect of sitting – God help him and us! – in a *window* seat without the reassuring presence and comforting words of his trusty companion. At the very last moment – he probably looked out of the window! – he had realized that, complimentary champagne or no complimentary champagne, he could not survive take-off without his mate and had ended up hyperventilating in the doorway of the aircraft. Needless to say, this had caused a bit of a commotion and was distressing for everybody else on the flight. Air-fright phobias, the cabin crew had realized, were potentially contagious and in danger of multiplying.

Having taken the gentleman off the aircraft, it took twenty minutes to calm him down and rearrange the seating on board so that he could be repatriated with his friend who had, by this time, resigned himself to being shackled to his nervous buddy for yet another business trip – and probably for life! From that day hence, I've always tried, whenever humanly possible, to avoid separating passengers from their companions.

Returning to the current problem, I decide that it will be easier – and possibly safer! – to upgrade both passengers to Business Class so that 28A and 28B can sit next to each other, rather than try to juggle the entire Economy Class cabin around. While the team leader instructs the staff about the seat changes, I leave the boarding gate, which is already beginning to fill up with people, in order to see how things are going on board the Ilyushin.

Having re-boarded our four-engined giant, it comes as no surprise to me to see that the cleaning supervisor is still running around like a headless chicken trying to hurry things along. Not wanting to add to the pressure she's already under, I adopt a diplomatic tone and ask, 'How we doing then, love? Is the sucker working on the carpet or not?' 'It is, Jeremy,' she replies, 'but we're going to be about another ten minutes here, I'm afraid. Is that all right? The rest of the aircraft is clear and the purser is happy.'

Ten minutes will mean only a slight delay to the boarding time, so I'm not overly worried and leave the staff to carry on mopping up the water while I go to see Igor. 'Gorskii, mate! The cleaners need another ten minutes, so I'm going to delay boarding until 10.35. Is that little ole toilet unblocked yet?'

As Igor turns to speak to me, I begin to appreciate the size of the problem! Two enormous rubber-clad hands, caked in all sorts of unmentionable things, come zooming towards my face. 'Do you mind, Gor!' I protest. 'Urgh … that's awful. I don't want to know what you've been doing with your hands, but it looks like you've found your true vocation, mate!'

✈ OVERLEAF 'You've got the shopping list, now don't forget the bust of Lenin – Stalin simply isn't good enough!' I run through the various loading information with the captain, ensuring that our flight departs safely, which is obviously paramount.

Igor is clearly trying to fathom out why he spent years studying aerodynamics and not plumbing, as he retorts, 'Jemskii, dearest Mr General Secretary, I've got just one thing to say to you – *Crapskii!* No, Jem, seriously, I can't shift this mess, but I have managed to stop the leak. However, I'm going to have to block the toilet off, and the guys in Moscow will have to strip it right down to fix it.'

Back at the gate, with people littered everywhere, it's apparent that things are going well! Strolling back towards the front desk, I'm convinced that there must be an air-raid taking place. The departure gate reminds me of the pictures I've seen of families living in the Underground during the Second World War. However, images of London during the Blitz are soon shattered by the sight of Russian children crowding around the vending machines and scrapping over chocolate and cans of drink.

A queue of people, clutching boarding cards and passports, has formed at the front of the lounge, and Simon from AFSL has joined us to oversee the AFSL staff. 'Ah, Jeremy, I'm glad you're back. The Hounslow Suite have been on the phone wanting to know when they should bring the Ambassador over to us. I said about ten-to, is that okay?' 'That's fine, Simon. Did they say how much baggage the Ambassador has?' 'According to the suite staff, his party has hand baggage only,' Simon replies in his usual calm manner.

I should explain that Heathrow is equipped with five specialist suites – the first being the Royal Suite, through which members of royal families and heads of state are handled. The four remaining suites are attached to each of the terminals, and you may be surprised to learn that they are not intended for use by film stars and rock bands. They are specifically for smoothing the passage of government officials, foreign envoys and other such categories of people through the airport. Sorry, no prizes for guessing that the Hounslow Suite is where VIPs flying from Terminal 2 are processed.

What do I mean by 'processed'? Well, in simple terms, someone such as His Excellency, the Ambassador of the Russian Federation, is never required to queue at check-in for his boarding card. Instead, he passes through the tranquillity of the suite and specially trained staff escort him and his party by diplomatic vehicle directly to the aircraft.

'Jemskii,' Igor says, 'we can go boarding now.' As virtually every Russian passenger stands ready to rush towards the exit, I make the all-important boarding announcement. Those of you who have flown before are probably familiar with the procedure of passengers being called forward by seat-row numbers or specialized zones for boarding. Well, forget that! This system is absolutely hopeless and never works when you're dealing with inexperienced Russian travellers. The minute I finish speaking over the Tannoy, a staff member opens the doors and leaps to one side as the passengers stampede down the jetty, making the charge of the Light Brigade look inconsequential.

After just five minutes, the lounge is all but deserted and Simon comes across to inform me, 'We're six down at the moment.' This is the best news I've had all day. We still have fifteen or so minutes to go before departure, so there's every chance things will come together in time.

I spoke too soon. My radio is hissing again. 'Jeremy – from Kasia.' The Tsaritsa is sounding a good deal less calm than an hour ago. Perhaps the fact that two Aeroflot flights are now simultaneously checking in (SU242 for Moscow and SU638 to St Petersburg) is having some effect upon her. 'Go ahead, Kashinka.' 'Jem, is there any chance of a Have A Go?'

Now, a 'Have A Go', or HAG as they are known to us, is a person who's arrived too late for check-in, but still wishes to try and catch the flight. Because the passenger is late, we can never guarantee that the aircraft will wait for them; and if they wish to have a go, they need to run all the way to the gate, towing their baggage. For this reason – and because some of the distances involved can be quite considerable – the passenger needs to be fairly fit. Once the HAG accepts the sprint challenge, they are given a temporary boarding card and sent on their way, on the understanding that they have not yet been accepted for travel.

As I stand visualizing a passenger with an enormous suitcase at check-in, I remember a story told to me by a colleague working for a handling agent at Gatwick Airport. One afternoon, this particular employee had just finished checking in passengers for a flight to Dubrovnik, when a young Croatian student came running up, desperate to get on the flight. After explaining that there could be no guarantee, but he could have a go, the passenger was sent with his bags to the gate. The check-in agent turned his back for a moment to obtain a HAG boarding card but was suddenly distracted by a commotion further down the row of desks. The young Croatian male, obviously misunderstanding his instruction, had leapt on to the baggage conveyor belt behind the desk and was heading, clutching his luggage, towards oblivion!

'Kashinka,' I say, snapping out of my reverie, 'we're nearly complete here, love, and should be departing on time. Has the passenger got much baggage?' 'It's a young English guy with a medium-size rucksack, travelling to Bangkok,' the queen of lipstick informs me. 'He should make it.' My spirits lift immediately. The guy is English, so there's little chance of any misunderstanding, and he's young, so should have enough puff in him to make it to us within the ten minutes left before departure. 'Okay, love. Send the passenger on a strictly on-chance-only basis, please.' Having received Kasia's confirmation that the passenger is doing his level best to impersonate Linford Christie, I turn my attention to the remaining passengers.

'How many are we down now, Simon?' 'Looks like two Russians are still missing,' the AFSL supervisor reluctantly informs me. The usual process of searching high and low for the two stragglers commences, just as the Ambassador's group arrives alongside the aircraft. Glancing through the window to check all is well, I see that both Harry and Boris are on the ramp seeing to the Russian delegation, so, thankfully, there's no need for me to leave the gate.

Exactly three minutes before the magic 11.00 departure, our HAG, a Mr Williams, arrives at the gate gasping for breath. I'm not in the least bit surprised that this passenger has reached us before the two missing travellers, who, incidentally, were the first two people to check in! The HAG is congratulated and issued with a boarding card, as Simon dispatches his newly labelled rucksack down a special chute to the ramp for loading.

It's time to let Igor know how we're doing. 'Gorskii, we've just sent the last bag down, so you can close the holds now, mate. Unfortunately, we're still looking for two female punters. I'll keep you posted.'

Just as I finish talking to Igor, my telephone rings: 'Is that Jeremy?' 'Yeah, it is. What can I do for you?' It's the Supervisor from the

Central Search area, who's phoned to tell me that there are two Russian women stuck in a queue at Passport Control, who are eagerly trying to make their way to us. 'Are they definitely SU248 passengers?' I ask, needing to make sure they are not travelling on the SU242 at 13.30. Sure enough, God love 'em, they are. Why they have only just gone through Passport Control is anybody's guess! Simon pre-empts my next request and sends a member of staff to find them.

Finally, at 11.23, the last two passengers stroll into the gate with the staff member, who has been desperately trying to encourage them to run. 'Gor, we're complete.' Having informed Igor that we now have a full complement of passengers, I can't resist asking the two women, in their early forties, where they have been all this time. After establishing that they don't understand a word of English, I repeat the question in Russian and am astounded by their reply: 'Well, you see, we checked in very early at eight o'clock, looked at our watches and decided there was still time to go shopping. We got the metro to Gammersmith [as Russians pronounce it!] – very nice shops – then got stuck coming back when the metro did not move for twenty-five minutes.' Incredible! I've just held up 307 passengers, including the Russian Ambassador, for two middle-aged Russian shopaholics. The saints preserve us!

No sooner has our mighty IL86 pushed back from the ramp for its three-hour-forty-minute journey to Moscow, than I hear Kasia, who has returned to the  office for a short coffee break, declaring, '241 zoning for Golf 14.' Fortunately, Pat, having been replaced by Kasia on the ticket desk, will be coming up to co-ordinate the turn-around of this aircraft, so I'm able to head straight for the office to prepare all the documents from SU248 to be sent to Moscow. However, before heading off to the office, I need to meet the arriving flight, which is very conveniently coming on to the adjacent parking stand.

The door of our Airbus A310 swings open and who should be stood there but our very own super-efficient Colonel Kleb. Phew! There is a God after all! Pat's now got the joy of keeping my dear friend, the Colonel, happy. 'Morning, Jeremy. We have 171 passengers on board and here are the in-bound documents.' As I nervously accept the paperwork from the in-coming flight, our business-like stewardess says, 'Relax! You're okay. I have all the bread rolls I need for the return journey.'

Hello ... has this stone-like goddess developed a sense of humour since Tuesday morning? Not wanting to test the waters any further, I confirm the expected number of passengers on the return leg and rush off back to the office, thankful for a near escape. Having survived nearly six full days on shift, I don't want to ruin it all by crossing the most efficient stewardess working for Aeroflot!

While the remainder of the terminal is collapsing under intense heat as a result of the wonderful weather outside, our office is paradise. The air conditioning has stayed faithful to the plight of the humble Aeroflot collective and will probably – before much longer – be awarded the Order of Jeremy. Igor, who is sitting at his desk enjoying a short break before the Tupolev TU154 arrives from St Petersburg, informs me, 'Jem, Heathrow Air Ambulance have been on the phone to confirm the arrangements for that doomed stretcher! Would you be so kind and call them? There were a couple of things they wanted to check'.

My heart begins to race. Up until now, I've managed to put the prospect of the stretcher to the back of my mind, but now things are becoming alarmingly real. Trying to conceal the tremble in my voice, I confirm to Comrade Engineer First Class that I'll call the ambulance guys as soon as I've had a cuppa.

Heathrow Air Ambulance is a private company that provides full medical assistance to airlines at the airport, in addition to the normal emergency cover offered by the London Ambulance Service. The company is responsible for bringing the passenger and attending nurse out to the aircraft in a specialized vehicle, which can be lifted up to the door, thus making the transfer of the patient on to the flight much easier. 'Hello there, it's Jeremy of Aeroflot concerning the St Petersburg stretcher passenger ... I believe you called.' 'Yep, sure did!' a cheerful guy at the other end of the line declares. 'I just need to confirm that the departure time is 14.25 and that the on-board stretcher has been organized.'

Now, strictly speaking, the flight should depart at 14.25, but what the ambulance operative doesn't know is that we're going to have to fit the stretcher when the aircraft arrives. 'Sure, 14.25 is correct, although there may be a slight delay. Could I ask you to bring the patient out to us at around 13.50, please?' The ambulance driver agrees and confirms that he will arrange for the patient and nurse to be checked in by AFSL over the phone. So far, so good, although I still have a nagging feeling that there's something not quite right about all of this.

As I start tearing off all the messages that have been coming through concerning the departure of SU248, I notice that SU242 has been given a departure slot time by the European Air Traffic Management Centre, Brussels. In simple terms, this centre has the difficult task of co-ordinating the flow of all aircraft in and around the European Union, and ensuring that the crowded skies above us are managed to the highest safety standards. To eliminate the possibility of an accident, they allocate departure slots to flights when traffic is at its peak and needs to be controlled. After all, there are only so many air traffic control officers, and they can handle only so many flights at any one time. An Air Traffic Management Centre, Brussels, slot should mean that the air traffic controller doesn't become inundated with aircraft all heading in the same direction at the same time.

'Patsy – from Base.' No answer. 'Patsy – from Base.' Still no answer. Pat's either got her radio switched off, or the Colonel is offering her up for a sacrificial burning. 'Patsy – from Base. Answer please, hon!' Thankfully she's still with us and replies, 'Go ahead, sweetness!' 'Patsy, are you all right down there? Is the Colonel treating you well? You've got a take-off slot of 14.00, with push-back at 13.40.' All's well at the aircraft, my cat-loving colleague confirms, and acknowledges the ten-minute delay to push-back. Believe me, ten minutes is nothing. There are occasions during peak periods when we can wait anything up to two hours for a departure slot to be granted by Brussels.

Everything appears to be going well for Pat and Harry down on Golf 14, and Kasia's been very quiet, so I can only assume that she's either busy dishing  out beauty advice in between issuing tickets, or she's fallen asleep from boredom. '637 zoning for Golf 12 everyone.' Clearly the Polish Empress was enjoying a peaceful forty winks as she states over the radio, 'D'you mind, Jeremy! There's no need to shout. You startled me!' 'That'll teach you, Kashinka, to fall asleep on the desk. I'm off with Igor to sort out the stretcher.'

The Tupolev TU154-B2, scheduled for arrival at 13.25 (sorry, folks, you can ignore the B2 if you're not an aircraft boffin, but, if you are, you'll know what I'm talking about!) is equipped with three Kuznetsov NK8-2U engines, which give off a very distinctive sound. So even before we can see the aircraft, we can hear it and know that it's going to arrive on stand just two minutes behind its 13.25 timetabled arrival. At 13.29 the captain switches off the engines and the steps are put into position by the second door of the aircraft so that the passengers can disembark.

Before I can go and brief the crew for the return journey, I need to inform the ramp team leader about the stretcher. 'All right there, how's you? When you're unloading, mate, you should find a stretcher. If poss, could it be brought upstairs to us, please?'

Working with my colleagues from St Petersburg is always a pleasure. There's something very special about the people from that glorious city. I'm not entirely sure what it is, but they seem friendlier than most.

Tanya, the Chief Stewardess, is standing in the doorway as I run up the steps. '*Zdrasvoi, no kak ty?*' she queries. 'All's well,' I reply. She's smiling from ear to ear. (She's obviously under the same doctor as dear old Aunty Pat and Igor.) I then brief the team about the passenger figures for the return journey.

This particular aircraft is equipped to carry 132 passengers in a two-class configuration, and we are expecting 127 people. Before I've had a chance to finish translating the crew's horoscopes from *Bella* magazine, a bit of a ritual with the girls on a Saturday, I'm interrupted by the team leader. 'Sorry, Jeremy, but I think you'd better come and take a look at the stretcher. It's not what you think it is!'

As I make way under the aircraft towards the front hold, I can see that SU242 is just pushing back for Moscow. Two flights down, just one more departure and an evening arrival to worry about. Standing next to a baggage conveyor belt is Igor, shaking his head in disbelief. 'What's up, Gor?' 'Jem, you *definitely* don't want to know!' In his hands are two long poles. Suddenly, I want the ground to open up and swallow me. 'Is that what I think it is?' I gulp, then add: 'No, don't answer that question. You're right – I don't want to know.' Igor is clutching a stretcher that looks like it's just come off the set of *Mash*. You know the sort of thing I mean – two poles with a strip of heavy-duty material strapped between them.

This truly is unbelievable! The man we are expecting has a suspected broken neck and I'm supposed to put him on a stretcher that has about as much support as a punctured life-raft at sea! Igor, overcoming his initial disbelief, enquires of the crew what exactly has gone wrong. Some bright spark in St Petersburg, it transpires, decided to slip this particular stretcher on board because the engineers were unable to fit the correct equipment. Seemingly, the person who loaded the stretcher thought they were doing us a favour by sending something less complicated! Give me strength! If the patient weren't in pain before getting on the aircraft, he certainly would be after flying for three hours bouncing up and down on this little delight.

Before we know it, the Heathrow Air Ambulance has arrived to start loading the passenger. Call me Psychic Sid, if you will, but did I not say that I had my suspicions about this so-called 'easy' MEDA case? Seeing the patient strapped flat on his back to a specialist stretcher, I get the feeling that a nightmare is about to emerge. Not knowing what to say to the ambulance crew, I offer a knowing smile and leave Igor to discuss the finer points of our predicament with them. Come on folks, give me a break here, I do need to go upstairs and check how things are moving along at the gate. Igor's a big boy, and quite capable of dealing with the current conundrum on his own for a few minutes.

Blast! Just my luck! All's well at the gate. The staff are coping wonderfully well, and nearly 120 of the physically fit passengers have arrived already. I have no excuse to linger and should therefore go back to the aircraft to see how things are progressing. Unlike the stereotypical military leader, who always arrives at the last minute to save the day and take all the glory, I arrive just in time to see a calm-looking passenger being lifted through the door of the aircraft. 'Gor,' I whisper, 'sorry to be a pain, but have we devised a cunning plan yet? Where on earth are we going to position the passenger? He clearly cannot travel on that ridiculous thing. Look, his head is all strapped up. I'm having very very bad vibes about this.' Igor doesn't answer, just keeps smiling, which is very worrying in itself.

The next moment, sorry, no ... I cannot believe my eyes. This isn't happening. Can this be for real, everybody? Somebody please pinch me. If I didn't know better, I'd think I was still asleep in West Drayton. Right before my eyes, the passenger with the broken neck is being unstrapped and helped off the stretcher into one of the Business Class seats! 'That stretcher, guys,' I gasp as the two paramedics turn and give me a puzzled look, 'can you take me away on it, please! I simply do not believe what I've just witnessed. That bloke is supposed to have a broken neck ... ' 'No,' Igor corrects me, smiling, 'he's broken his hip and has been kept flat with his head strapped down as a precaution.' No time to stand and stare: I'm suffering from post-traumatic stress and need to find a doctor for some of those happy pills.

As I go back up to the departure gate to make the announcements, the ambulance drives off. 'Now listen everyone,' I say to the flight boarding team, 'I don't want any missing passengers, or people who've lost mobile phones, carrier bags, etc. No children with hands stuck in those blessed vending machines. No pregnant women suddenly deciding to check out my midwifery skills – and definitely no missing musicians giving impromptu concerts around the terminal. I'm a man on the edge! Do I make myself clear? After my latest experience in the Twilight Zone, I've decided I need a very long holiday far away from here.' At first, the relatively new staff members are not sure whether I'm being serious or not and listen with worried looks on their faces. 'Actually, Jeremy, we're complete,' somebody dares utter. With the theatrical drama-queen flair of Victor Meldrew I say, 'I don't bloody believe it.'

But it's true. At 14.03 all the passengers have arrived. A miracle, which makes up for all the hassle I've been having so far today. For the first time this week, I'm able to close the doors to one of our flights ahead of schedule. All 126 able-bodied passengers, plus one seemingly fraudulent medical case, are aboard with ten crew members and 3.5 tons of baggage and cargo. Exactly four minutes ahead of schedule the aircraft is gently eased back by the tractor unit and I wave goodbye to yet another Jeremy nightmare.

The girls laughed for ages after I retold the delights of stretcher travel, and were still chuckling as they left for home about twenty minutes ago. Pat and

Boris will both be back in the office tonight to meet the arrival of SU582 at 19.45, and Kasia will be busy playing bridge with her husband and a couple of friends. As for Igor … Well, he'll probably sit and watch some really bad third-rate movie and make us all re-live the experience tomorrow morning. Yours truly needs to get ready for Dave's little shindig.

The journey to Dave's takes just twenty minutes and I arrive in the leafy suburb just after 6 p.m. clutching two bottles of Mother Russia's elixir of life, vodka!

'Please do come in, General Secretary, sir! Mate, you look shattered.' 'Thanks, Thomashenko. I thought I'd done a really good job covering that up!' Unbeknown to me, Dave has gathered up some of my old colleagues from Czech Airlines, as well as his entire family, but I'm so tired I can hardly keep my eyes open. After just one glass of wine, I'm dead on my feet. 'Humble apologies, everyone,' I say, 'I'm going to have to be a real a party-pooper and head off home. I'm on again in the morning, and still have to do battle on the M25.' Declining Dave's kind offer for me to stay the night – I need to see to Lenin and Rasputin – I make my way home.

Just after 8.30 p.m., while I'm lying in a nice hot bath trying to block out all thoughts of medical passengers, it suddenly dawns on me that tomorrow is going to be a *really* long day. Not only do I have three flights at Heathrow to worry about, but I also have to go to Stansted in the evening for the first of a series of twelve extra Sunday flights from Moscow.

Time to hit the sack. After all, I'll be lucky to be in bed much before midnight tomorrow …

CHAPTER 7

HALLELUJAH! TRANQUILLITY AWAITS

THE WORLD IS A TRULY BEAUTIFUL PLACE this morning. Although I've yet to run the gauntlet of three fully booked flights from Heathrow, and face the ensuing hordes arriving at Stansted this evening, everything seems to have a glow of optimism about it. Nothing can convince me that the world is anything other than beautiful – not even if I find myself with a flat tyre during a thunderstorm on the M25! So good am I feeling, that I've managed to stir myself from a deep relaxing sleep – one that was free of feline nightmares – at 4.45 a.m. before the alarm clock has even had a chance to find its voice. Why, I hear you ask, am I sounding so euphoric? Simple, folks. It's Day Seven! Hallelujah! There's a bright light shining along the tunnel of my stressed life, and at the end of today two days of tranquillity await me.

As I negotiate my way through yet another set of traffic cones, which, incidentally, have sprouted overnight, my cheer is momentarily distracted by a debate on the radio. 'God intended Sunday to be a day of rest …,' comes the slightly pompous voice of a vicar

SUNDAY

✈ Sunday at last. I believe I could take on anything in the world today – everything seems to be going smoothly. There's even time to relax and talk to the plants in the lounge. It's good for them, so I'm told. Not even the arrival of flight SU 241 can spoil my day.

165

who obviously feels passionately about shops opening on Sundays. 'Shop staff – like everyone else – should be given the opportunity to give thanks to God on Sundays,' he continues.

Hang on a minute! Am I missing something here? I dislike mobile telephones intensely, but I'm beginning to regret I don't have one to hand so that I can call the radio station to offer my opinion. I would love to know which day the vicar thinks God intended airline industry employees to rest and give thanks? Why is working in a shop any different from being a policeman, train driver, or, for that matter, a cheerful airline traffic supervisor? Fortunately, another member of the radio panel, who also happens to be a vicar, has seen the light and is offering a counter argument. Indeed, so convincing is his rationale, I can switch channels and listen to some classical music. Rather appropriately, Dvorak's *New World Symphony* is playing. Many people associate this delightful piece of music with the Hovis bread commercials, but for me it's a chance to lose myself in the wonders of reaching Day Seven with my sanity almost intact.

07:10 Walking along the first-floor concourse towards the office, I get the feeling I'm the only person who's made it to Heathrow this morning. It's blissful. The terminal is all but devoid of travellers, and only the occasional security announcement is disturbing the peace. Where is everybody? Perhaps the hordes have decided to give us a miss today for some reason.

But no such luck. As I pass the entrance to W.H. Smith, a long train of people, who look as though they are attempting to dance the conga together, start coming up the escalators from the ground floor. At the head of the queue is Gabichka, who doesn't look best pleased. 'You all right, Gabichka?' I enquire. 'I need to get my breakfast before I answer that question, mate!' my Polish colleague replies. 'Fair enough, Gabs. Are you going to get yourself an almond croissant? If so, could you get me one, too, please?' Looking rather drained, Gabi heads off in the general direction of food. I dash off to the nerve centre.

Just as I'm unlocking the door to the office, Patricia comes round the corner. I'm not sure what's up, but she appears to have lost her Cheshire grin from yesterday. What if she got home last night and discovered that one of the kittens really had gone AWOL on me on Friday night? No … don't be silly, Jeremy, she'd have called last night to say something was amiss.

My head is spinning with all kinds of possibilities, so I decide better to ask than to sit in fear that she's discovered a head-count discrepancy at home. 'Patsy, are you okay, love? Gabs isn't looking too happy this morning either. Have I done something wrong?' A big mistake this last remark! What if I've done nothing untoward, but she now starts to think I've got a good reason to feel guilty. 'Morning, sweet! Nothing's wrong. I just didn't get a lot of sleep last night. Don't forget I was here for the night stopper, and then stupidly sat up at home watching a late-night film on Channel 4.' Phew! All's well with the cats … I told you Sunday was a beautiful day.

Having shared the early-morning duties with Aunty Pat, and having left Gabi to finish filling her face with an almond delight, the full impact of what may  be ahead has hit me. The three flights from Heathrow are going to generate more than 800 passengers, which can mean only one thing – lots of hassle! On the first flight alone we are expecting around fifty-seven transit passengers via Moscow for Dhaka, many of whom, from past experience, will have excess baggage problems of gargantuan proportions, but no money to pay.

On top of this, we have a flight from St Petersburg to Gatwick and the extra evening service from Moscow to Stansted. This aircraft, being the first of the twelve extra flights, will thankfully be all but empty on its return leg to Moscow – just seven passengers to look after. Not wanting my energy levels to peak too early, and because I'm only too aware of how things may develop during the next six hours, I've volunteered to man the ticket desk for the first flight, leaving Gabichka and Aunty Pat to deal with operational matters for SU581 to Tokyo via Moscow.

Before ensconcing myself at the 'Show Case', I decide to take a short detour to check-in to ensure all is well. As I do this via the great outdoors, I'm afraid it's definitely a case of once bitten twice shy. The memory of the hordes of people milling through the building early yesterday morning is enough to convince me that my chosen outdoor route is the best option if I'm going to avoid high blood pressure so soon into my last day of duty. As I head along the front of the terminal building, my face raised to the early morning sun, I catch a glimpse of the growing queues in front of Swissair and Iberia's check-in desks. It's not a pretty sight, believe me. In fact, so ugly is it that I'm almost tempted, from fear that our own check-in will look just as unpleasant, to go back to the office and seek refuge behind my desk.

My fears are justified. Numbers are already building up at our check-in and the staff are looking frazzled. Glancing along the five desks, I get the distinct feeling that something's not quite right. Now, let's see. I should have four Economy Class and one First/Business Class desk. Okay, that's what I've got. All the display screens behind the desks should be showing SU581. That's also in order. So what is it, then, that's making me feel something's adrift here? I double-check: the First Class desk is looking resplendent with its carpet and barriers, but ... wait a minute! Where's my flower display gone?

Sitting behind the desk is a very sheepish-looking Ash, who normally greets me with the latest airport gossip. 'Hi, Ash. Did you not bring the flowers out with you?' 'Jeremy,' she answers, trying to raise a smile, 'they've gone missing, I'm afraid. They weren't in the COP first thing. I've asked around and no one knows where they are.'

Some explanations are due to you here. Since the introduction of the flowers nearly two years ago, I've had four displays severely damaged through alleged accidents, and at least six complete displays lost without trace. Every time a display vanishes, my imagination runs riot, and my theory that Heathrow's Twilight Zone really does exist is

---

✈ What's this we have here, then? Excess baggage? No, just checking that the labels are in fact for my flight and that the check-in staff are not too harassed by the swarms of passengers and their luggage. It's just like the *Generation Game* on this conveyor belt!

reaffirmed. But, if the truth be known, the flowers could be going anywhere. Perhaps an undertaker, down on his luck with a cash-flow problem, is sneaking in late at night and purloining them for future business engagements? Maybe there's a thriving black market in airline flower arrangements and Heathrow has got its very own flower-power Mafia bent on ridding the airport of its floral tributes? Who knows? All I care about is how I'm going to find the time to replace the blessed things – and chain the new ones to the counter!

'Ash, I'll be over on the ticket desk if there are any problems. Pat will be down shortly to join you.'

As I make my way through the sea of people, I can see a group of about twenty of the Dhaka passengers standing around the scales, frantically checking the weight of their baggage. Looks like I'm going to be busy issuing excess tickets, especially as Patsy will be co-ordinating check-in and, as you know, she takes no prisoners! Fortunately, there is no one waiting to be served at the ticket desk, so I'm able to get everything ready in peace.

 With less than an hour remaining for check-in of the first flight, Pat is beginning to get miffed with the Dhaka passengers, who are refusing to book in. At this point, I should explain one of the oldest tricks in the trade for passengers with too much luggage. They seem to have the idea that if they wait until check-in's on the verge of closing (normally thirty minutes before the scheduled departure time), they can then pounce on the staff who, in the last-minute panic, will check them all in, waiving any charges for overweight baggage because time has run out. How wrong they are! If there's no time to process their excess baggage payments, they're simply refused permission to travel!

Aunty Pat, of course, has been systematically informing all the stragglers that this *is* our policy, but it doesn't seem to be having the desired effect on them. Things are relatively quiet on the desk. I've issued only three TODs (remember this little code – Ticket On Departure), as well as giving out endless tips about the best way to reach central London by public transport.

Just as I look up again at the Dhaka masses surrounding the scales, a large gentleman, looking very shifty, approaches me. He's sweating profusely and constantly adjusting the collar of his tight-fitting shirt. To make matters worse, he's clutching a small package close to his chest! I've seen those airplane disaster movies, too, you know, and read those suspect-package posters, and my heart is beginning to pound! How can I best deal with this would-be terrorist? I know! Try to look as cool as a cucumber and act like I suspect nothing. Easier said than done. I've obviously not got the right kind of blank facial expression to convince this Mohammed Ali lookalike because, in a deep guttural tone, he asks, 'Are you all right? You don't look so good!' When, tongue-tied, I do not immediately reply, he adds, 'Can you help me, please, I have a big problem?' I'm sure he has, but so do I, and I've never been on one of those Samaritans' courses, so I don't know how to begin convincing him that being a suicide bomber is not the answer!

Desperately trying to mask my concern, I begin to chat with this awesome-looking man. 'I'm fine, sir, just very tired. How can I help you?' The moment I finish speaking, he reaches inside his jacket and I feel myself beginning to sweat and flinch uncontrollably. Getting shot on Day Seven is not high on my list of priorities – even though it will make good television if the film crew's around!

Suddenly, however, everything's clear. He's no terrorist, thank God. He's a member of Aeroflot's staff based in Brazzaville (the People's Republic of the Congo) and is holding a space-available staff ticket, which means he must stand by and wait in the hope that fare-paying passengers will fail to turn up to travel. I'm right about one thing, however. He is very nervous. He's cut his return journey home very fine and his boss in Brazzaville has warned him not to be late back to work.

If you are one of those people who thinks that receiving a free staff ticket is an excellent perk, you might be surprised to learn that staff travel is fraught with nightmares that the average person could not begin to comprehend, let alone deal with. Seeing this rather pitiful-looking colleague in front of me reminds me of the times I have sat in various airports around the world wondering whether I would ever get on a flight.

On one occasion, I had to spend a night curled up on some very uncomfortable chairs in Vienna, having been denied boarding on an already full Austrian Airlines flight to Johannesburg at just after midnight. On another occasion, I spent three days at Kai Tak Airport, Hong Kong, desperately trying to get back to London during a typhoon! Every airline was chocker with people and all the hotels were full. Kai Tak was bursting at the seams for days with airline staff from all around the globe trying to do the same thing as me – escape on a staff ticket! Absolutely exhausted and dirty, and vowing never again to travel on a free ticket, I eventually made it home.

Such experiences – and vows – are soon forgotten, however. A year later, in 1992, I was stuck with my sister and nephew in Sofia, Bulgaria. We had just spent ten wonderful days in the Maldives and were forced to return to London via Sofia because the direct flights were so busy. We arrived in Sofia on a Friday to a temperature that was already minus fifteen degrees centigrade, and found there was no connection to London. Spending the night in a seedy hotel in the centre of Bulgaria's capital after ten days in paradise was not exactly appealing, as you can imagine. Anyway, having survived a taxi journey from hell, during which the driver spent most of his time with his head under the dash-board trying to fix the heating, we reached the airport to discover the flight to London was horrendously overbooked. My sister promised to keep calm, but the prospect of having to wait until Monday was beginning to show on her face.

While I was trying to negotiate our passage with a very unhelpful female at check-in, who, by the way, was sporting a thick black moustache that would put any man's to shame, my sister and nephew were cuddled up together on a wooden bench. Sitting next to them was a guy who resembled Worzel Gummidge. This poor unfortunate was wearing summer clothing and a pair of hessian sandals.

As I returned to update my sister with the latest information, the Worzel lookalike was asking her, 'Do I need visa for London? I don't have, but I good boy – want work. Easy job – find or not?' The man, who was in his late fifties, was obviously slightly barking! After fifteen minutes of further incoherent questioning, he suddenly got bored, stood up and walked off. By now, my sister was utterly convinced that she had been sitting next to a recent release from the funny farm. Anyway, when at last we managed to get on the flight, guess who was sitting immediately behind us? Yes … Worzel. But we never did find out what happened to him when he arrived at Heathrow without a visa!

'Don't worry,' I tell my staff-ticket colleague from Brazzaville, 'I'll do all I can to get you on the flight, but you will have to wait until just before 10.30 when the last few passengers have checked in.' As my enormous colleague leaves looking slightly less anxious, a few of the Dhaka passengers, who have just grasped that Aunty Pat isn't joking, have gathered to pay their excess baggage charges. Of the fifty-seven people transiting to Bangladesh, twenty-three have more than 10 kilos each of excess. 'Patsy, how you doing over there, hon?' I call. 'They're still stood here expecting a miracle to occur!' my dishevelled colleague responds. 'I've sent a few over to you to pay, but at least fifteen of them are still arguing the toss – and pushing everyone of us over the edge!'

I notice that one of the passengers waiting to pay me is shaking his head to and fro. 'Is there something wrong, sir?' I enquire, thinking that he's getting impatient at having to wait in the queue. 'No, no, young man,' he replies. 'I just cannot believe how my fellow country-men behave at times.' Slightly taken aback by his response – having half expected him to hurl complaints at me – I commiserate. 'To be honest, sir, I feel the same when I see how some Englishmen behave on holiday. It's always the minority who give the wrong impression.' After just twenty minutes, the queue dissolves and I'm able to sit and compile my preliminary sales report.

Gabi has already positioned herself at Gate 40 (yes … the gate that matches the aircraft parking stand Echo 40). Poor Gabichka! She'll probably need  new shoes after trekking the equivalent of Heathrow to Hounslow and back). Pat has gone for a well-earned rest in the office before coming down again to staff the ticket desk. With only thirty-two minutes to go before SU581 is due to leave at 11 a.m., I finalize my sales report and go across to check-in to close the flight.

My Brazzaville colleague is patiently standing by check-in, although he's clearly been sweating buckets while waiting. His clothing is absolutely wringing wet and the parcel he's still clinging on to is now sodden. Two desks down the line there are three transit passengers still arguing with the staff about baggage: 'Twenty years we travel Aeroflot and never before we pay excess. Always we have 35 kilos each.' I step in to save the check-in agent having to explain the rules for the fiftieth time this morning. 'Well, I must say, sir, you've been jolly lucky over the past twenty or so years to have got away without paying. I'm terribly sorry you think we are so unpleasant in London, but you have taken so long to decide about paying for your bags that, I'm afraid, we simply have to refuse to accept you for travel.'

The language that ensues is so vile that I'm unable to put it into print for fear that my book will attract an X-rated certificate from a censorship board. Being a rather large chap, and incredibly thick-skinned, I'm able to ignore the torrent of abuse with ease and turn to address my Brazzaville comrade. 'Okay. You're in luck. These three gents have very generously donated their seats to your plight, so I'll be able to put you on the flight. You'll need to run all the way to the gate, though!'

My colleague is truly overwhelmed and, as a thanks-offering, thrusts the small dripping package he's been nursing into my hands. In that now familiar deep tone of voice, he states, 'Thank you very much, you've saved my life. If you are ever in the Congo, please call me in the office. Enjoy the chocolates, please.' There! Would you Adam and Eve it? He's given the game away! I was hoping to be able to host my very first game show, called *Guess the Gift*, back in the office. The winner would, of course, have received the dubiously damp contents of the parcel!

Thanks to the three very articulate gents at check-in, my vocabulary of obscenities has grown two-fold since 10.30, and, ooh, it's now only 10.45! Continuing to hurl abuse at me and vowing to return – doubtless with renewed vigour – next week, they pick up their baggage and leave me to face the queue of passengers now forming for flight SU242 at 13.30.

Thanks to an air-traffic control slot, flight SU581 left for Moscow and Tokyo just twelve minutes behind schedule at 11.12 a.m. Gabi has now taken up position in the office and is busy answering the phones in between preparing her post-departure report for head office. Patsy, in the meantime, has been kept busy trying to persuade a few overweight Russians (no, not enormous great shot-putting types, but people with too much baggage … *el surpris*) that they need to part with their last few pounds sterling to pay their excess luggage charges. She appears to be having varying degrees of success, and the stress of not being able to speak Russian is beginning to show on her face as she draws yet another picture for two avidly watching passengers of two strapping great blokes struggling to lift a suitcase with 100 kilos written on it! It really is marvellous, don't you think, how – when all else fails – drawing pictures or making outlines in the air can overcome any language barriers?

Queues at check-in are now stretching way beyond the main entrance and Heathrow Airport's staff are desperately trying to usher passengers into the correct lines for check-in. In the distance I can see several British travellers getting slightly animated with the frazzled staff. It looks as though I'm not the only one who's having to take a flood of abuse from short-tempered travellers. Stress management on days like this can be very difficult, especially when you are leaping from one check-in desk to the next dealing with passengers' problems.

While I'm busy explaining for the hundredth time that passengers can take only one small piece of cabin baggage weighing no more than 5 kilos with them, a well-dressed Russian lady approaches me. 'Excuse me, are you the Aeroflot representative?' 'Yes, I am, madam. How can I help you?' Without hesitation, speaking in English in a soothing voice, the lady informs me, 'I'm head of the Moscow Youth Choir and we are here for check-in. Where should we go?'

✈ OVERLEAF Still waiting for flight SU241. While doing so, I decide to read to Claire and her AFSL colleague from Tolstoy's epic *War and Peace*. This could be the record…we've reached chapter two already!

Having established that there are thirty young singers needing to be processed through the system, which is already showing signs of cracking, I move the group to one side of the hall and ask someone from AFSL to open two designated group check-in desks. This choir is not the only group I'm expecting today, so having designated desks should, in theory, speed up the processing of all the passengers.

Just as the choir master – oops, should I say 'mistress' here, or perhaps 'person' would be more correct? – hands me the group's tickets, I turn and say with a large grin on my face, 'I'm terribly sorry, madam, but we cannot check you in at the moment!' Naturally, the head of the youth choir is puzzled by my statement and asks, 'Why? What's wrong? Is something not in order?' Above the ever-increasing din of irate passengers yelling about baggage, I reply, 'Nothing's really wrong, I just have my suspicions that the children can't sing. Before I can check you all in, I need convincing, I'm afraid!' The Russian choir leader (yep … that's probably the best way to describe her), who looks very much like Bet Lynch in *Coronation Street*, smiles as she realizes I would simply love to hear the group sing for us.

Suddenly, finding her voice, she booms, 'Get ready, children. We have to sing for our boarding cards!' On that note, the children stand still, almost to attention I would say, and simultaneously begin clearing their throats. 'Do you have any special requests?' asks the Russian. 'Do they know any English songs?' I reply. 'If so, I'm sure the whole terminal would love to hear them sing, although, personally, I would prefer to hear a couple of traditional Russian folk songs, if possible.'

No sooner said than done, the choir bursts first into a rendition of 'Rule Britannia'. Silence engulfs the check-in hall as the choir lifts the spirits of every Brit in the building. The choir has done what no man could do before: they have succeeded in calming down all but the most ferocious among us. Everyone is clearly moved by the experience. Like larks, the children continue with their own version of 'Greensleeves'.

Just as I begin to think they are going to finish without singing a single Russian song, they stir themselves for a rousing rendition of 'Moscow Nights', which many of the other passengers know. Suddenly every Russian in the Aeroflot check-in area is singing along with the choir. For all-too-brief a moment, people seem contented and at peace with themselves. Excess baggage, what's that? No non-smoking seats left, who cares? Alas, the singing comes to an end as Gabi declares over the radio, '241 zoning for Fox 15,' and the hassle of trying to process more than 300 passengers relentlessly plods on.

Marina, sitting at desk 22, calls out, 'Jeremy, could you pop over here for a sec, please?' Regretfully, as I do not possess the voice of a lark and do not wish to  embarrass myself in front of the talented children from Moscow, I resist the temptation to sing my usual tribute to my AFSL colleague. 'Marina, love, what's up?'

Standing in front of the desk is a middle-aged gentleman dressed in an Armani suit. I know what you're thinking! How on earth do I know he's wearing an Armani suit? Well, that's simple. He's holding his jacket over his arm and the label is protruding slightly! And, before you ask, he doesn't really strike me as the type of person who needs to demonstrate his wealth. 'This gentleman,' Marina says, 'has come across from Terminal 4. He should have travelled to Moscow this morning with British Airways, but there was some kind of problem with his visa.'

Surprisingly, it's not uncommon for people to arrive at check-in without the necessary documentation for travel. Often people receive incomplete information or are misled by others who claim to be experts on travel requirements. Sometimes people become so con-fused that they don't know what is needed for a particular destination. I recall hearing a story of an elderly lady who was visiting her son in Australia for the first time. She presented herself at the Qantas (Australian airline) check-in desk in Terminal 3 and was duly asked to produce her passport and visa. After several minutes wrestling with the zip of her handbag, she withdrew her passport and newly acquired Visa Barclaycard and plonked them on the counter. When questioned by the bewildered check-in supervisor, the somewhat confused lady replied, 'My travel agent said I needed a visa, so I applied for one from my bank. What's wrong? I don't understand. Isn't it the right kind of visa?'

✈ We've tried CPR but to no avail. I think the best thing for it now is twenty minutes in boiling water and then to be served on a bed of lolo rosso. I don't know whether I've convinced Catherine, but excess baggage can produce the odd surprise.

Strictly speaking, check-in should have sent the lady off to the Australian High Commission to obtain the necessary entry visa, but through the efforts of the Qantas staff she was allowed to travel to Sydney, where the authorities issued her with the correct documentation.

'Good afternoon, sir!' Our visa-less Canadian national turns and smiles at me as he explains that his company, based in Toronto, has arranged for his Russian visa to be made available to him upon arrival at Moscow's Sheremetyevo 2 Airport. Because British Airways have been unable to verify this information, they have been forced to adopt the correct procedure of denying the passenger carriage. I should mention at this stage that it's a passengers responsibility to arrive at the airport in possession of all the required documents, i.e. visas and health certificates, etc. 'I'll see what I can do to help, Mr Klein,' I say. 'Can I just see your ticket, please?'

I know this may sound a daft request to you, but if I *am* able to obtain confirmation that Mr Klein's visa will be awaiting him in Moscow, he will probably ask me if I can accept his British Airways ticket rather than make him purchase an Aeroflot one. Sometimes, however, it's simply not possible to take another airline's ticket for use on our flights. For example, passengers who have paid a very low budget fare will normally be restricted to travel with their original airline. Fortunately, though, Mr Klein is holding a full-fare Business Class ticket, so all I need to do is send a telex to our colleagues in Moscow to check that all's well with his visa.

I arrive at the ticket desk just as Aunty Pat is handing over the reins to Gabichka. 'Sorry to interrupt, girls, but could I ask one of you to send a message to the visa section in Moscow to check whether or not they are holding a visa for a Mr Klein? Here's his passport.' Pat is heading off to Gate 15 to supervise the departure of our second flight, SU 242, which is due to leave in just under forty-five minutes at 13.30, so Gabi agrees to do the necessary. 'I'll give you a shout over the radio, mate, once Moscow reply.' Thanking Gabi, I fight my way back through the ever-growing queues to explain what's happening to Marina and Mr Klein.

Still no news from Moscow about Mr Klein's visa. Unfortunately, for the second time in a day, the Armani-clad Canadian has come up against the

forces of time and motion. Regretfully, I'm unable to permit him to travel on the 13.30 flight. Check-in closed for that flight twelve minutes ago, with 314 passengers on board – just two people shy of a full complement. Check-in for the next flight now continues apace, as a group of 300-plus Russians arrives for flight SU244, which is due to leave for Moscow at 3 p.m. I've been away from the office since 08.30

this morning and it's time for me to take a short break back at the nerve centre to gather my thoughts. Bidding Marina and the gang farewell, I advise Mr Klein that I will do all I can to get him on to the last flight of the day. The passenger thanks me for my efforts and I dash off in a bid to maintain my sanity.

On my way back to the office I'm collared by a group of Russian women sporting the ubiquitous carrot-coloured hair-do. They are desperate to know where they can obtain their VAT refunds. Explaining what they need to do takes me longer than is necessary because most of them are not paying the blindest bit of attention to anything I am saying, except to the word 'cash'.

Eventually they grasp that if they want to get their mitts on more of those lovely notes with the Queen's head on, they need to listen care-fully! Finally, at 13.35, I manage to break free, only to hear Patsy's voice on the radio, 'Jem, are you anywhere near the info desk? If so, could you make an announcement for me? I'm just two kids down at the moment! Usual story, I'm afraid. The teacher allowed them to wander off to do some shopping, and then couldn't find them.' I oblige my colleague, and as I leave the relative calm of the information desk, I bump into my old mate, Igor, who informs me, '243 is going to Golf 12, mate. Are you coming with me?'

'Excuse me, Gorinskii,' I say, 'is this one of those real-choice test thingys? The 244 is due to leave in about an hour and fifteen minutes, so, once again, no coffee break for me. D'you know something? I must have been really wicked in a former life to be deprived of even the simplest pleasures in this one.'

On the way to the gate, Igor and I spot one of Pat's boarding team trying to find absconders from the 13.30 SU242. Knowing how Russian kids love their burgers, I ask, 'Have you tried McDonalds?' Sure enough, just two minutes later, the AFSL agent reappears with hamburger absconders in tow. As they rush past us, the out-of-breath staff member shouts down the radio, 'I've got them!' Glancing down at my watch, I see that Pat's flight is complete just eleven minutes behind schedule, at 13.41. I told you today was going to be wonderful. We've already managed to send more than 500 passengers on their way to Moscow. It's all downhill from here.

'Jeremy – from Gabi.' 'Yeah, go ahead, Gabs.' 'I've just had a reply from Moscow about Mr Klein,' Gabi's excited response comes over the airwaves. 'All's well. Someone from the visa section is able to meet him when the aircraft lands.' 'Excellent. Can you make sure Mr Klein is checked in for me then please, Gabi? The only spare seats are in First Class, so you'll need to upgrade him.'

As Igor makes his way on to the ramp to meet our mighty Ilyushin IL86, which is just pulling on to the parking stand, I wander off to the boarding gate to get things rolling for the departure.

Just five minutes ago, a miracle occurred and I'm still pinching myself to make sure I'm awake. What happened? Well, every single passenger, including  Mr Klein, arrived at the gate ten minutes ahead of schedule and all the cargo and baggage has been loaded. Somebody somewhere is looking after me on my last day. Whoever it is, I'd love to thank them for making Day Seven such a pleasure.

Looking through the window on to the ramp, I can see that Igor is shutting the hold doors and that the main door to the passenger cabin has already been closed. So, for the first time today, we're ready to depart ahead of schedule.

At exactly 15.00, the aircraft's anti-collision strobes (red flashing lights) start to flash. This tells me that the captain has received clearance to push back from the ramp for the three-hour forty-minute journey to Russia's capital. It's just possible that I've discovered the equivalent of the mysterious happy pills that everyone in our office has seemed to be on over the past couple of days. I can feel a huge beaming grin forming on my rather large face. Just think, I've been wandering around for over ten years trying to work out how to keep smiling and the elusive answer's been staring me right in the face – a flight that comes and goes on time with the minimum of hassle. Simple, wouldn't you say? Makes me wonder why I never twigged it before today. Such is life!

Suddenly my Cheshire Cat grin slips. Why, I hear you ask, am I not feeling so good all of a sudden? Answer: the captain's just switched off

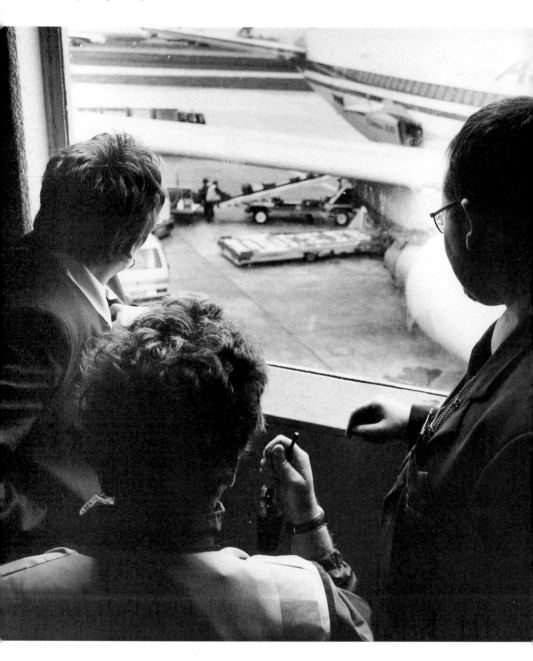

✈ Here I am again peering down on to the world below me, this time with Aunty Pat and Catherine (the dispatcher). We seem to have an incident and it's drawing a bit of a crowd. It turns out that there's more baggage than even I could have predicted. Thankfully, though, skilful planning on my part means that no one will be without their smalls in Moscow.

his anti-collision strobes! Something's up! I don't believe my bad luck. Just when I thought I'd found true happiness, someone or something has come along and pulled the rug from under my feet.

'Gorskii – from the Gen Sec.' Igor, standing behind the glass and struggling to unclip his radio from his belt, gesticulates that things are not going according to plan. A moment later, he says: 'Jemskii, it looks as if one of the engines is jiggered!' My heart sinks. This simply can't be happening to me. Doubtless, I was very wicked in a former life, but *why* should someone decide to pay me back *today*? Couldn't it have waited until another day when my energy levels are at top speed?

For twenty minutes, Igor battles to rectify the problem with the starter motor on engine number one, but, regretfully, has to admit defeat. 'Jem – from Gor.' 'Go ahead, mate.' 'This is no easy fix, I'm afraid,' he tells me. 'Moscow will have to send me the necessary spare parts as they're not the sort of stuff I hold here on station.'

This means only one thing – a long delay. I'm not talking an hour or two, I'm talking anything upwards to five hours. Why so long? Well, we have to wait for the spare parts, known as 'AOG' spares, to arrive. (Yes, the codes keep rolling in! AOG = Aircraft On Ground, and AOG spares are acknowledged by every airline in the world as an urgent shipment on its way to assist a crippled aircraft downline from its operating base.) Our AOG spares will now need to be loaded on to the extra flight to Stansted, and Igor will have to collect them, then return to Heathrow to repair the Ilyushin IL86.

According to the information he has just given me, once he has the spares on site, it will take up to an hour to fix the problem and he will then need to run the engine a couple of times to make sure all is in working order. So, to be realistic, this delay could last anything up to seven hours! For Aeroflot in London, such technical problems are, thank the Lord, very unusual. But why, oh, why, has this rare event happened now at the end of my shift? A delay of this nature is regarded as one of the worst possible nightmares for any airline!

You could be forgiven for thinking that I'm defeated and about to give up the fight. After all, this engine trouble is worthy of being con-sidered the last nail in my shift's coffin. Wrong! This is just the sort of challenge I love. I thrive in the face of adversity; thrive on having to kick in with a contingency plan to minimize the effects of such delays for passengers.

Adrenaline is coursing through my veins at maximum speed; my tired state dissolves into the buzz of having to think quickly. While Igor goes off to the office with the flight engineer to call Moscow and arrange for the AOG parts to be loaded on to SU241B, which is due to leave for Stansted in just over thirty minutes, I turn my attention to the passengers. The moment has come when I need to face the wrath of more than 300 hungry travellers, whom I'm quite sure have recently graduated from a vampire's course in Transylvania! Am I about to be rendered anaemic?

 The answer is no. My Russian passengers really are a delight to work with, you know. As I explain that something is wrong with the aircraft, they simply thank God that we've discovered it. Many of them say, 'Don't worry. We understand the situation. We would rather wait for things to be fixed.' How refreshing! An elderly couple, who have been in London on their first-ever overseas trip, approach me and say: 'Young man, thank you very much for explaining in Russian exactly what is wrong. Delays are common in life, so why worry? We all know that, eventually, at some point, we are going to leave. Some of us are even grateful for the opportunity to stay a little longer in this beautiful country.'

Yes, I can always rely on Russians to be philosophical about problems. I love them! Unfortunately, the non-East European passengers, including poor Mr Klein who, it seems, will never make it to Moscow, are somewhat more displeased with the news. Thankfully, however, only one passenger pipes up with a string of abuse that puts this morning's three Dhaka passengers to shame!

You will probably have gathered by now that it's essential for me to think on my feet all the time. Who knows what's around the corner? During my speech about the aircraft's problems, I've devised a cunning plan to minimize the delay for the passengers. I will transfer them by bus to Stansted, where they will be able to join the six or seven passengers who have booked to return to Moscow on board the almost-empty SU242B, which, incidentally, is also an Ilyushin IL86. At least that way the pressure on Igor to work himself into the ground will be reduced, and the out-going passengers will feel as though we are trying to do everything we can to assist.

What's involved? Well, that's not so easy to explain. First, I have to arrange for the passengers to be kept in the lounge, while I return to the office and organize everything. Thankfully, Heathrow Airport's security staff are on hand to assist my AFSL colleagues, and the passengers are kept in the gate lounge with light refreshments. Back in the office I brief the rest of the staff. Pat then organizes six coaches to transfer the passengers to Stansted, while Gabi liaises with Immigration and the handling staff at AFSL to escort the passengers back through Passport Control so that they can board the coaches to Stansted. 'I'll go and sort out the baggage transfer, Pat, and then come back to collect all the passenger manifests, etc.,' I say. 'Could you give GHi [our handling agents at Stansted] a call and tell them what's happening? I'll send them all the telexes they need when I come back for the paperwork.'

Leaving Pat and Gabi frantically co-ordinating the passengers, I go to brief the AFSL operations staff, including the ramp operatives, who will have to unload the baggage from the aircraft to a large truck for sealed transfer to the Essex airport. (The bags, which have already been through Security and X-rayed, have to be kept in a secure environment.)

In little over an hour, we have managed to arrange six coaches, two trucks for baggage, the transfer of all the catering supplies from the crippled aircraft into  trucks for the hour's journey to Stansted, and the processing of more than 300 people back through the Immigration area. Pat and I are now seeing off the first two coaches from outside the Queen's building at Heathrow, while Gabi and Harry are informing Moscow what decisions we've taken. The Moscow staff will need to keep meeters and greeters at their end fully informed, as well as arrange for transportation to take the passengers into the city centre. Moscow, like London, does not have a twenty-four hour public transport system, and the flight will arrive at Sheremetyevo Airport just after 2.30 a.m. (Moscow being three hours ahead of Britain).

'Pat, I'd better go back to the office, collect all the out-bound paperwork and then get myself to Stansted.' My flagging colleague agrees and, as I leave, continues to count the passengers on to the remaining coaches. It's essential that we have exactly the right number of people travelling to Stansted. We certainly don't want to lose one on the way!

Back in the office, things have moved on nicely. Harry has gathered up all the paperwork for me and arranged for extra staff to act as receptionists at Stansted when the coaches arrive. Before zooming off to Essex, I check that the in-bound flight is operating on schedule, which, thankfully, it is. In fact, the aircraft should be touching down at 18.55, slightly ahead of the planned time, so Igor (who is in his own car) and I need to get our skates on. Igor will need to grab the AOG parts the minute the aircraft arrives on the parking stand and then zoom off back to Heathrow. We've both got a long night ahead of us. We really are a pair of poor unfortunate fools – perhaps because we joke too much!

Driving round the M25 (for the last time this shift, hooray!), I manage to overtake all the passenger coaches, but, unfortunately, there's no sign of the baggage or catering trucks. I can only keep my fingers crossed that they will arrive in time. They were, after all, the first vehicles to leave Heathrow.

 My visits to Stansted Airport, which I think is one of the world's best-kept secrets, are normally such a pleasure. I pull up in this peaceful part of Essex to find the staff eagerly awaiting the arrival of the coaches. Immigration are on stand-by, having been briefed by their colleagues from Heathrow, and I'm informed by the GHi supervisor that the baggage has been at the airport for about twenty minutes. Thank you, God. I definitely don't want anything else to go wrong now. I'm not sure I could conjure up any more adrenaline if something else decided to collapse at this point.

While I wait for news of the aircraft's impending arrival, I manage to sneak the first ten-minute break I've had all day. The sun is slowly moving off to the west and Stansted looks almost romantic. Perhaps my vision is blurred by sleep deprivation – who knows? My coffee break comes to an abrupt end as the flotilla of Aeroflot-chartered coaches pulls up alongside the terminal. Like an army of ants, the passengers file out of the buses into the building, where the staff are waiting to assist them through Passport Control. Fortunately, GHi at Stansted employ a Russian national, Galina, so she's able to assist with any translation, leaving me free to head off to meet the aircraft.

At precisely 18.55, the third of today's mighty IL86s lands in the United Kingdom. I stand patiently watching the 307 in-bound passengers come off the flight and, yes, my mind does begin to wonder what kind of problems they might create when they leave in several weeks time! Igor has already grabbed the AOG vital components needed at Heathrow and has said his goodbyes.

Eventually, twenty minutes after the aircraft door first opened, the last of the passengers disembarks and the cleaning crew go on to spruce up the cabin for the return leg. It's time for me to break the bad news to the crew. They had all been expecting an easy ride home, with just seven passengers to look after. Although they know that an IL86 is on the ground at Heathrow, they had expected the passengers to be kept there while repairs are carried out. How wrong they are! They soon have it confirmed that you can never take anything for granted!

'I'm sorry everyone, but I'm afraid I've got some bad news.' 'No, don't tell us,' the Chief Stewardess interrupts. 'We have all those delayed passengers coming back with us!' Now, here's a staff member who would do really well on my game show *Guess the Gift*. I nod, then encourage them to carry out their pre-departure checks. Making my way on to the ramp to check that the fuelling truck has arrived, I'm pleased to see that the caterers are already loading up all the trolleys.

Although the sky has gone a very deep shade of black, the nightmare's coming to an end. Just three minutes late, I manage to account for every single passenger, bag and meal. The cargo that should have gone on the IL86 has been left at Heathrow and will be loaded on tomorrow's lunchtime service to Moscow. I'm now able, for the last time today, to bid another of our crews farewell. Grudgingly, they thank me for my efforts and, for the second time in five hours, the door is closed on our now extremely tired travellers.

As the airbridge is removed from the aircraft side, the heavens open. Now when I say open, I mean a torrential downpour. Raining cats and dogs doesn't even begin to describe the rain now pouring down from on high.

Nothing's happening, except the captain's doing a good impersonation of Igor by gesticulating at me through the cockpit window. He then struggles with the handle and shouts through the rain, 'Runway closed at the moment due to the weather.' Aaah, never! I don't believe my luck. Not content with upsetting me at Heathrow, God is now testing my patience to the limit at Stansted. I've just survived seven full days of a shift, which has ended with *the* nightmare to end all nightmares, and now I'm faced with the prospect of another delay. If the aircraft is held up for more than an hour, I will have to off-load everyone and put them up in hotels until the morning as the flight will not be able to land – Moscow Airport's runways are closed for repairs between 4 a.m. and 7 a.m!

Turning to my GHi colleagues, I say: '*Please* – just push me off the end of this airbridge right now! I can then spend a few weeks in hospital away from all of this madness.' The GHi dispatcher assures me that it's going to be a short shower and that all will be well. As I glance across at the aircraft, I'm convinced I can see steam rising from the heads of the passengers.

'Matt, can you advise Jeremy that the worst of the rain is beginning to subside and the airfield is opening again in a few minutes?' This news from GHi's Control Room is music to my ears. I'd almost lost the will to fight on. Six minutes later the aircraft pushes back, and I breathe a sigh of relief.

Back home, I feed the cats and have a long soak in the bath to unwind. While I'm lying there, it dawns on me that you have now come to the end of your journey through *Jeremy's* Airport. Tomorrow you'll be able to return to the land of logic, and the events in the Twilight Zone will become a distant blur in your memory. I, on the other hand, have just two days to unwind before tackling the next marauding crowd. I can't wait – no, seriously, no sarcasm this time. Give me the wonderful world of Heathrow any day.

Just before we part company and I wish you all a safe onward journey through life, I would like to ask that next time you are standing somewhere in an airport about to lose patience, please remember our time together and spare a thought for all of us in the industry. As I'm sure you've learned over the past seven days of sharing my life, what happens – and sometimes what doesn't happen when it should – is not always our fault. See you at Heathrow!

Bon voyage – and happy landings …